CRAIG'S RECORD FACTORY

A Young Entrepreneur's Journey Through the 70's and 80's

CRAIG ODANOVICH

www.Holon.co

ISBN#: 978-1-955342-21-6 (Hardback)
ISBN#: 978-1-955342-23-0 (eBook)

Published by:

Holon Publishing & Collective Press
A Storytelling Company
www.Holon.co

I would like to dedicate this book to:

Cathie, my beautiful wife! You have stood by my side for forty-one years and raised our four beautiful children, all while finding time to forge your successful career.

Cathie and me in Craig's Record Factory

And to Steve and Jane, my loving parents, on whose shoulders I stood to spread my wings and fly!

(Left to right) My parents, Jane and Steve, my sister, Cherry, myself, and my sister, Jan.

Introduction

I have been asked over the years if I had ever thought about writing a business book. The idea never appealed to me. It is a crowded field with thousands of terrific stories by very accomplished professionals. With some prompting by a publisher, I revisited the idea. As I mentioned, my story is no better than others. Still, I realized what might be unique is the fact I went into the record store business at the age of twenty in 1972, when the industry took off. That journey led me to the video rental business in 1980, which WAS the beginning of the videotape recorder, which made it all possible. Two long gone, golden eras.

I could keep these separate yet unique cultural times alive through my writing. Fellow baby boomers can relive and revive their memories. At the same time, any of their descendants, if they so choose, can learn about these golden times. Just maybe, it will shed some light on who their parents and grandparents are. Anyone that is not an entrepreneur and always wondered what it was like might follow my exact footsteps and share the experience.

I had a terrific group of people join me on this journey — competent people with a shared vision and genuine allegiance to a common goal. I have always had the philosophy that it is imperative to always do what is in the best interest of the business entity, not an individual cause. That was my beacon and allowed me to make hard decisions along the way, such as letting people go. I asked myself, is this in the best interest of the business and the other people who were working so hard to make things a success. Shared success is so much more rewarding than individual success. That was a lesson I learned in my basketball days.

In this book, the reader will find themselves exploring small town life, beginning in the fifties. High school hangouts, jukeboxes, and living by the Gulf of Mexico. They will follow my footsteps as I opened a small record store and grew the business until opening my pride and joy in 1979: CRAIG'S RECORD FACTORY! Then we will transition into the video rental industry at its very beginning. We went head to head with Blockbuster and won. Then there's my time as the Executive Vice President of Hollywood Video. We will wrap up with a few chapters on the writing of my trilogy, The Black Widow Trainer, and its subsequent screenplay. The book chapters are full of excerpts to give the reader an example of my writing style as well as a feel for the storyline.

It is an unconventional journey. I had no college degree, but a good understanding of business from observing my father in the family-owned Dairy Queen. I never plotted my future, simply followed the path laid before me. Never applied for a job, yet worked for large enterprises. But more importantly, this is a book about the times I lived and the people who shared the experiences.

It is about business, but it isn't a business book. Business is the thread that leads the reader through the exciting time of rock and roll, promoting concerts, muscle cars and video rental stores. Having already written a fictional trilogy in my fifties and currently shopping the screenplay, my new goal is to write a nonfiction novel, keeping it light and enjoyable. If the reader walks away with ideas to run a better business, then so be it.

Contents

"Little GTO"
— The Beach Boys

On a warm summer's day in August — 1969, while riding with my dad to get a new car, I contemplated the summers I worked in my family's Dairy Queen. Since the age of fourteen, summers entailed working seven days a week, ten hours a day. The only shortened day was when I went to church with my family on Sunday mornings. I never gave it a second thought or complained, as both my mother, Jane, father, Steve, and sisters, Cherry and Jan, worked just as hard. It was now time to reap the rewards!

I had no clue what I was looking for, so we toured the Pontiac dealership's lot. There were plenty of choices, like the fine silver Firebird with a 326 HO engine. The salesman asked us to come to his office to visit. I was thinking the Firebird was the one, until I walked past a sweet baby blue 1969 GTO right outside his office. Could it be a sign? Taking a closer look at the beast, to my surprise, the GTO was equipped with a 400 cubic inch, 350 horsepower engine and a honking Hurst 3 speed shifter on the floor. But would my dad go for it? 400 cubic inches is much more muscular than the 326 cubic inch Firebird. But why bring it up? He was a grown man. Let dad do his own research. I held my breath as he wrote out the check for $2,995 plus tax (no, we did not use words like 'sweat' and 'honking' back then, but hey).

I pulled into the driveway of our home, which was across the street from my parents' DQ in Flour Bluff, Texas. It was a big hangout spot for high school kids since it opened in the early 1950s. Fonzie would have been proud. Walking over to the

DQ I saw my friend Roy Smith. Roy immediately launched into how he was at the Pontiac dealership a few days ago. He told me all about this beautiful baby blue GTO. Did he not see me pull into the driveway? Apparently not. Grinning and pointing to my house, I said, "Do you mean that GTO?"

I allowed Roy to be the first person to ride in my car. No, not just a drive around the block — zero to sixty on the back roads of Flour Bluff Drive. Hitting sixty in second gear, I power shifted to third gear, and the Goat jumped towards eighty, then ninety, then 120. I was too busy watching the road to see Roy pinned back in his seat. Five-point nine seconds from zero to sixty was Roy's official time. Had I laid a $100 bill on the dashboard in front of Roy, I'm not sure he could have reached it.

It was the age of the muscle car. They roamed the streets as godlike beasts, looking for wheels of prey. Mustangs, Goats, Superbees, Barracudas and Road Runners. Now it would only be a matter of time before they came looking for me. I promised myself I would never challenge another car, but what I would do if challenged? Only time would tell.

"Happy Days Are Here Again"
— Annette Hanshaw

My love for music began at age four in the back of my father's Dairy Queen. Opened in 1954, it resembled those old joints with the gigantic ice cream cones on a tall pole. The DQ parking lot had metal poles with sheets of tin metal to give the cars shade and protect them from the elements. Students from Flour Bluff High parked in the lot on Friday and Saturday nights, hanging out with their friends like at Arnold's Drive-in in *Happy Days*. They filled the back room, loading nickels in the jukebox and dancing.

As a young tyke, I spent many a night in a comfortable chair situated behind the jukebox. The sound was almost as loud as if I had been on the other side. Songs like "Rock Around the Clock" (Bill Haley), "Tutti Frutti" (Little Richard), and "Don't Be Cruel" (Elvis) were among hundreds of others that filled my head — never to escape, as I found out later.

Several years ago, I listened to the Sirius Radio '50s channel over three days to see how many songs I recognized. It was close to ninety percent of them. Have you ever stopped to wonder how our brain retains the melodies and lyrics of thousands of songs as if it were a hard drive? Millions of recorded songs to date and millions more to come. From only twenty-six letters in our alphabet come millions of lyrics, all different from their predecessors, all telling a different story. Notes are constructed in a unique way to produce so many cords and riffs. It's simply astonishing.

Flour Bluff was an un-annexed community that lay between

Corpus Christi, Texas, and North Padre Island. The DQ was the last business in the Bluff as you paid your toll and crossed over the causeway to the long stretch of fun in the sun. If you got lucky, you missed waiting for a barge to pass through the Laguna Madre channels, a body of water between the Bluff and the Island. Beaches with miles and miles of cars that were parked right up to the Gulf of Mexico, shores teeming with thousands of rowdy occupants enjoying a wonderful sunny day. Cool breezes blew in from the gulf to keep the ninety degree temperature with ninety percent humidity bearable. If that didn't work, cold beer and soft drinks did the job. Surfers preferred the proximity to Bob Hall Pier, where the massive logs supporting the long fishing pier provided surfable waves. The most daring of the lot surfed in the wake of an approaching tropical storm or hurricane.

The students from Flour Bluff High were a unique blend of fisherman's kids, blue collar workers, laborers, and Navy brats from the local naval air station, with a few white collared workers mixed in. And then there were the students bussed in from Port Aransas, a fishing community at the far end of the adjoining Mustang Island. Everyone in south Texas refers to it simply as Port A. Looking back, it was a proud community and functioned as a cohesive unit. The school board members had the best interest of the kids at heart. There were Whites, Blacks and Hispanics, but no one thought of race back then. They were just called Orlando Martinez, Charles Grey, Toby Heron or Woodie Jelks. They were just fellow students who we knew by name, not ethnicity.

The high school boys were rough and tumble in the early fifties and sixties. Many a fight broke out at the DQ between kids from Corpus Christi looking for adventure, swabbies from the naval base, Bandidos passing through, and sometimes (but seldom) amongst each other. Tuff guys like Calvin Self and Ronnie Babinaux will live in infamy.

But there was no match for my dad — an ex-tank commander in WWII, six foot one and 210 pounds of muscle. Steve Odanovich made sure there was no fighting during the day. Most of it happened after the DQ closed. But one Saturday afternoon, an unsuspecting group of motorcycle riding Bandidos pulled into the lot. They were looking to settle the score with Calvin and Ronnie, who weren't there, so they started picking on the friendly Bluff boys instead. At about ten years old, I was standing in the Dairy Queen, watching. The tension was ratcheting up when out of the corner of my eye, I spotted my dad headed straight for the 250 pound leader. He jabbed his meaty hand and finger into the Bandido's chest until he was backed against his bike. Steve stepped on his foot, pointed his finger into the leader's face, and gave him the same glare that kept me from acting up as a child. I noticed my Uncle Bud, also 250 pounds, coming over from our house as back up. To my amazement and amusement, the big guy got on his bike. Revving his hog loud, he motioned for his cohorts to follow as he screamed away. I found it somewhat interesting that although the Flour Bluff boys were tough, they never won many football games. Probably from a lack of discipline.

The stories are aplenty. One night some kids turned their car lights on two Bluffian's ready to duke it out and surrounded the match. One of the kids told a story about how someone grabbed him by his belt and shirt. The next thing he knew, he was flying through the air as my dad made a path to the center. That was the end of that. Or the time someone loaded the DQ air conditioning unit on the bed of their pickup truck. Dad sprang from our house across the street, with his old WWII rifle in one hand and holding up his pajama bottoms with the other. Dropping to the ground, he pointed at the culprits and yelled, "Drop it or I'll blast you!" And they did. Or the old accordion telephone booth where my dad spotted a kid he didn't want my sister Jan dating, talking on the phone. Knowing Jan was on the phone across the street when he left for the DQ, he became suspicious and wedged his body into the escape route. Jan never heard from that boy again. Later on, Willie Nelson filmed *Honeysuckle Rose*, and they paid my dad $100 for the use of the phone booth in the filming. Dad never cashed the check, just pinned it on the wall in the DQ.

"Father of Mine"
– Everclear

Dad grew up in Crosby/Ironton, Minnesota as the son of an immigrant mother and father. They left Croatia for America at the turn of the century, passing through Ellis Island in 1898. They were Serbian and came to work in the iron ore range. Mining was a hard life, but Grandpa Mike and Grandma ran a boarding house on the side. When the stock market crashed in 1929, they lost their life savings when the bank went under. Twenty thousand dollars was a lot of money in those days. But life went on through the Great Depression, and they had four hungry mouths to feed. My dad was the second oldest to Joe Odanovich, with Paul and Robert (Chubby) next in line. Dad learned English in the first grade, but he learned it well and there was never a hint of his old language. I remember playing on the floor as a kid one day, he got on the phone and began talking in a language I had never heard before. You can imagine my shock. He was speaking long distance with his parents, which was expensive in those days. Dad spent a few years in the Civilian Conservation Corps in northern Minnesota (CCC Camps), work programs the US government provided to help citizens get through the depression. After coming home, he went to work with my grandpa in the mines. I believe this is where he learned about capitalism. The mine workers were unionized, but Mike convinced the executives to let he and my dad, who worked in tandem, be paid by the carload of iron ore they filled. They made more money than the hourly wage miners through hard work and effort.

All four brothers served in World War II, and fortunately all four came home. The local paper ran a story about how my grandparents gave all four boys to the war effort. Their first cousin, Mike Dobervich, was in the 1st Marine's when the Japanese attacked Battan. He survived the Death March just to spend over a year in the concentration camps. I believe it was the toughness he experienced growing up in the mining town that gave him the courage to be one of the only eight Marines to escape. One by one, they were taken to Australia on submarines, while the others stayed back and fought with the Philippine resistance. As a hero he toured the United States, helping to sell war bonds and then returned to the Philippine Islands with General McCarther because of his extensive knowledge of the area.

Dad was such a good clerk that his commanding officer wouldn't let him go to war. The officer told him that he would spend the duration of the war under his command. Dad went over his head to the commanding officer of Fort Snelling, who knew him from his CCC Camps days. The commanding officer wrote a letter on dad's behalf, which dad's reporting officer then threw in his face and told him to get the hell out of his sight. He caught a troop carrier to Europe in time to be part of the final push across the Rhine to defeat Hitler.

Dad was much more than the DQ bouncer. He was a businessman in the truest sense. When he opened his Dairy Queen in early 1954, no DQ had food. Founded in Joliet, Illinois, the Midwest chain only served soft serve ice cream for about seven months per year — closing for the winter. The original Whataburger on Weber Road had only been operating for about four years. Whataburger is now a regional chain, which is in the process of going national. Dad loved a good hamburger, so he decided he would add a grill and fryer. I'm not sure if Dairy Queen ever sent a representative to Corpus Christi. I'm sure they felt this franchisee dropped out of the sky and as long as we made our royalty payments on the ice cream mix on time, that's all they needed to know. My best guess is we were over one thousand miles from the next closest Dairy Queen.

Dad named his version of a Whataburger, the KC Burger. Years later I asked him why, and he said Texas drove their longhorns to Kansas City in the old days so the beef could be shipped all over the country via railway. As far as I know I was the only one to ever ask that question. You can tell he was fiercely independent by the way he added food and never told Dairy Queen. I spent time in Morton, Illinois to visit my daughter, Michelle, and the grandkids. Their neighbor across the street had owned the local Dairy Queen since 1951. After telling him the story of my Dad and the KC Burger, he said that he had begged Dairy Queen to let him serve food but got nowhere. The best I can tell, the first DQ Grill and Chill restaurant opened in Chattanooga, Tennessee, and they began advertising Grill Burgers on national TV in 2005. I'd say Dairy Queen missed the boat by about forty-seven years.

I don't think our burgers were (just) like Whataburger's. Dad had an attention to detail and wanted to make the best burger possible. Every morning before the DQ opened, he would make a trip to Moody's Meat Market. Mr. Moody would save the trimmings from the best cuts of meat and mix in chuck for the juiciness and added flavor. Because the patties were made fresh every day, there was no need for any type of preservatives. The next stop was the local roadside produce markets on Ayers Road, where Dad hand selected the tomatoes, among the other vegetables. We were instructed to cut out any of the white rind and only leave the ripe meat of the tomato. We had a specific process for grilling the burgers. The buns were basted with butter and toasted on the grill. Once the meat was flipped and the salt and pepper added, we placed the cheese on top and laid the bottom of the bun over it to trap the moisture from the burger. The top bun needed to be spread with mustard or mayo all the way to the edges, and the vegetables were generously applied.

It didn't stop there. The crinkle cut fries were dropped into peanut oil, and he made sure the oil was changed before it got bad. He sourced large hot dogs that would be crunchy on the outside after cooking, and dropped them in the peanut oil to cook. When they floated to the top we knew they were done. The crispy, juicy dogs could be covered with his homemade chili if the customer wished. Fishermen from as far away as San Antonio made sure to stop for a burger on their trips to the coastal bend. You see, we were a burger joint first and an ice cream shop second, although many a burger went out with a milkshake. I learned from my dad that nothing was too good for your customer!

Fun fact: When we opened, burgers were twenty five cents, cheeseburgers were thirty five cents, fries were fifteen cents, and drinks were a nickel or a dime.

"We Are Family"
— Sisters Sledge

Mom's family came from Hancock, a small town in Western Minnesota — population under 1,000. Her grandfather, Michael Bahe (the family always referred to him as Papa Bahe), opened the local newspaper in 1900. Papa grew up in Faribault, Minnesota, and I remember a story that was told about the time he was seven years old, standing on the downtown streets, and Jesse James, his brother, and the Younger Gang rode by on their way to Northfield. The Great Northfield Raid was made into a movie in 1972. My granddad, Jack West, and grandmother, Vivian West, took over the newspaper for Papa Bahe. Jack helped my dad get the loan to build his Dairy Queen.

My mother was a very caring person. She attended to our needs while first holding down a full time job at Flour Bluff Elementary School and later working the same hard hours in the Dairy Queen as my father. She was very religious, most if not all of our ailments were handled through prayer. Where my dad was a good businessman, she was terrific with customer service, treating ALL customers equally. They complemented each other well. Yet I doubt they ever complimented each other. My folks weren't big on hugging, kissing, or telling you they loved you. But their actions told a different story. There is nothing they wouldn't do for us, and until I married into a family of huggers, I didn't even realize our family was different. I imagine it was because they were raised by stoic parents and grandparents who weathered the Great Depression.

Where dad's family were war heroes, mom's family tree led back to Sylvanus Thayer, the father of West Point. Slyvanus turned the college into a first-class institution after being sent to France by James Madison to learn from their generals at the Ecolé Military Academy. When he landed, Sylvanus was disappointed that the general he was there to see, Napoleon Bonepart, had just left for a place named Waterloo! But he stayed and learned from Napoleon's generals and studied the academy's curriculum. Armed with over a thousand books on war strategy and civil engineering, he came back to take control of West Point. Of course the books were all in French, so learning the French language was made mandatory for the cadets. I visited West Point and had my picture taken underneath his statue. Sylvanus Thayer is my sixth great uncle. He was never married.

My sisters, Cherry and Jan, were seven years and five years older than I was, respectively. We ran in different circles, as you can imagine. It was more like different worlds. Working in the Dairy Queen together, we were always so busy there wasn't much time to communicate, and they were home doing their studying by night. Both made pretty much straight A's, Cherry going on to be valedictorian her senior year and Jan coming in third. The family thought Jan sabotaged her GPA late in her senior year because she was too shy to give the speech. I don't think I will ever forgive my sisters for setting the bar so high. Most of my teachers had taught my sisters and assumed I would be as good a student. It wasn't that I couldn't have made A's, I just wasn't willing to put in the effort. I wasn't big on homework after going through a whole day of school, and I pretty much never actually studied for a test. I just relied on what I had been taught in class or read in a book.

"School's Out"
— Alice Cooper

The '70s brought with them my final semesters in high school. My buddies and I doubled up on Friday night poker games at John Visosky's house. After a long night of playing cards, we stood lined up in his driveway to see who could pee the farthest. It's amazing the bladder control an eighteen-year-old has. Ashley Winship would occasionally stop by to play while drinking a bottle of Mad Dog 20/20. Ashley was like Joe Btfsplk, the kid in *Li'l Abner* with the black cloud following him everywhere. One night at the poker game, Ashley finished his bottle of Mad Dog 20/20 and headed home early. As I drove home in a dense fog, I saw a car nose down in the ditch. I could tell it was Ashley's by the tail of his car, which was sticking high into the air. I stopped to see if he was okay and to offer help, and Ashley said, "Nah, I'll just sleep it off where I'm at."

Another time on a break outside the band hall, a group of us were talking when we noticed Chester Maples, a lanky Ichabod Crane-like classmate running with Ashley in hot pursuit. I'm not sure what Chester did to Ashley, but it wasn't received well. Ashley's face was beet red. Chester managed to keep just out of reach of Ashley by using his long legs to his advantage. We were laughing at the spectacle and egging Ashley on when suddenly he disappeared from the face of the earth. We were awe-struck and dumbfounded, but within seconds Ashley exploded into the air yelling, "Arrggg," totally covered in excrement. Someone had left the top of the septic tank off. My sides hurt the rest of the day, as did everyone else's.

Flour Bluff was known for their basketball teams. I often had my parents or sister drop me off at the home games. One particular year we had a good team, and at mid-season a freshman named Gilbert Walker transferred to Flour Bluff. Gilbert was Black, athletic with incredible ball skills, and an engaging personality. The team was very good before he arrived but this catapulted them to the top of the standings and into the playoffs. I followed them as far as they went. Players like Billy D'Herdy, Tosser See, Rene Curiel, Brian Stamper, Ray Torres, Gilbert Walker, Eddie Gowens ,and Pat Jones were gods to me at the age of fourteen.

I played on some very good teams myself in eighth and ninth grades. But we lost our coach, Bud Grey, my sophomore year, and although I made varsity, our team was no better than 500 over the next two years. But my senior year it was like the boys were back in town. Orlando Martinez, Earl Monroe, and I had played together for years. Actually, Earl had left for two years but was back for our senior season. We had a sophomore named John Sebastian move to the Buff who played solidly at guard, and then the icing on the cake was Bill Fette — all six foot five of him, which was tall back then. I won't bore you with blow by blow details, but we won district and bi-district. We lost by a few points the next round, when out of the blue our coach decided to change us from our normal style to a pressing style and told us to shoot from the outside, eliminating our inside game, which was very good. But the overall result was a 25-win, 6-loss season, setting the school all-time record. It wasn't until many years later that I looked back and thought that just maybe there were kids like me in junior high following us the way I followed Gilbert Walker's team.

I can't leave this chapter without another GTO story. We

were getting ready to play the winner of a playoff game. Coach Beard wanted us to watch the game on Friday night and scrimmage a team in Katy, Texas, that Beard had connections to in his early coaching days. Cypress Fairbanks, the team that we scrimmaged, wound up coming in second at the state tournament. Coach Beard owned a Cadillac, told the dealership he wanted to test drive another one, and then asked me to bring my GTO. The team loaded up in the three cars and headed out. The first leg of the journey was on a two-lane country road, as it cut off a lot of distance. Along the way, we could see Coach Beard in the lead Cadillac attempting to pass a car, but every time he tried, the car sped up as if playing with him. This game went on for a while until he finally got by. Then it was the second Cadillac's turn. The driver used the same tactic, and it took about five minutes to pass. Now it was our turn. By then, my teammates were boisterous and pissed off with the guy. As I pulled out to go around the vehicle, I stayed even with him long enough for my teammates to show him their middle fingers. Then I stomped on the pedal and pulled away instantly.

Team building, camaraderie, and playing in front of large crowds went a long way in giving me the confidence I would need later in life. Probably more than any course I took in school, other than maybe the ninth grade typing class, it prepared me for the future. Who knew computers were coming?

"Wasted Days and Wasted Nights"
— Freddy Fender

I don't think most of my buddies were going to college because that's what we dreamed of doing our whole lives, but we felt it was the right thing to do. My sisters, Cherry and Jan, went to a private college to the tune of $4,000 a year, which was a lot for those days. I carried a solid B average without studying and had the third-highest SAT score in our class. I had no worries of passing if I put in the effort. Still, the thought of retaking pretty much the same courses I took during high school for the first two years before I could make it to business classes was not appealing. Hadn't I just escaped all those English classes with Miss Aven?

I don't even recall my parents discussing college with me. Did my dad think I would work with him at the family Dairy Queen until I took over one day? Did my mother not want me to leave home, or did they figure I would go since both my sisters went to college?

I decided to follow my buds to a small four-year school in the nearby town of Kingsville. Was it because we were in the middle of the Vietnam War, and I needed a college deferment? I'm sure that factored into my decision. I like to think that if World War II had failed and our country were in danger of being run by Nazis, I would have gladly signed up on my own. But Vietnam? What was the point? That said, I have high regard for anyone who represented us over there. I wasn't keen about wasting my parents' hard earned money, and Texas A&I (now Texas A&M) would be much less expensive. Not wanting to feel bad — even at those prices — if I didn't do well, I came up with a plan. I asked my parents to pay me $500 a month ($1.66 an hour) working in the family business over the summer months, so that I could use the money to pay for my college, and they agreed. Now who could fault me if I didn't do well if I was using my own money? As it worked out, the $1,500 paid for my college tuition, books, lodging, food, and gas for my GTO. During the school year and in the summer I would live off the $300 I got back from tax withholdings.

It was my final summer before leaving for college. Luckily, my father wanted some of his land filled in, and the city of Corpus Christi was cleaning out the ditches in the Bluff. Dad bought an old dump truck and the city filled our truck for free. I spent my summer days hauling dirt, and I was happy about it. I enjoyed the solitude and the feeling of accomplishment as the low-lying areas of his acreage filled in.

One summer night, I went out with some friends to a small concert held at the StarDust Roller Cade. My friend, Steve Morgan, was a drummer and was mesmerized by the band's drummer that was playing that night. I enjoyed their music and thought they might have a future, but I didn't give it much thought. When we left the ZZ Top concert, we drove to San Antonio just for the heck of it, listening to Lee Michaels along the way.

At the end of July, Hurricane Celia sat off the Gulf Coast, stalled. Celia's projected path was Houston. When I went to bed, its sustained winds were only around ninety miles an hour — barely a hurricane. But in the morning, my mother woke me, saying Celia had changed directions and was headed our way. I was a veteran of riding out previous hurricanes Carla and Beula. Celia at the time was no more than a category one or two storm, so I called my buddies,

Greg Smith, Orlando Martinez, and John Visosky to come over to play poker through the storm.

When they arrived, we decided it would be fun to hop in Greg's truck and drive down Laguna Shore Drive, which was pretty much at the Intercoastal Waterway. The water from the Laguna Madre rose towards the road, which is not surprising. A little later, we noticed the telephone poles were starting to move. Greg had brought a hard hat he used working at his dad's cement plant, so he put it on and stepped out of the car to check things out. As soon as he was out, the wind blew his hard hat off, and it went rolling down the road. I can still remember Greg chasing after it with one of those green street signs caught on his jean leg. It was a cross street, so both street signs crossed. Laughing heartily, we began to realize this storm was more than what had been predicted, so we headed back to the house.

Back home, we settled in for our poker game. Things were fine until our large flat porch roof at the front of the house began waving up and down. It was supposed to be connected to the large concrete slab underneath with a metal pole, but my dad had not gotten around to bolting the round cylinder into the concrete. The roof rose and fell, the metal post hammering into the concrete each time, making a pounding sound. We stood there looking out our picture window in a trance, not quite believing what we were seeing. At about the twentieth time, the eighteen by twenty-eight foot roof sailed off. We ran to the back picture window and watched it twirl over and over until it was out of sight, as if it were a scene out of *The Wizard of Oz*!

By then, our Dairy Queen across the street was entirely out of sight, and my mother was in her bedroom praying. We turned up the radio. Celia was now a category three hurricane with sustained winds of 127 miles an hour. When the eye of the storm passed over, we stepped outside to assess the damage. We looked across the street to a demolished Dairy Queen. Nothing was standing but the side brick walls, grill, and ice cream machine. I was pleased I had not gone to a private college because my dad did not have insurance back then, and I'm sure it took his savings to rebuild. We went back into the house and braced for the backside of the storm to slam into us. We later heard small twisters were moving through the storm, and we were relieved one didn't hit the house. When we went out after the hurricane, we passed the neck of a trailer that had gone completely through a palm tree.

Nothing for me to do, so Bill Bryant and I took a trip to visit my grandparents on Lake Minnewaska in Minnesota. Twenty-four hours straight on two-lane roads. Passing cars was not a problem. It was a great break before heading off to school in September.

"I'm - *Not* - a Believer"
— The Monkees (...and me)

The following two years of school were a blur. I spent one year at Texas A&I, then half a year at Stephen F. Austin in East Texas, and the last half back at Texas A&I. Stephen F. Austin was just too far from home. Unlike the Navy kids who rolled through Flour Bluff in three-year stints, I was fortunate enough to attend the same school from kindergarten through twelfth grade. Over the years, I developed some great friendships that I carry with me today. Part of me envied the Navy kids that moved every three years. They were better equipped to shake it off and make new friends. But what was the depth of the friendships, and did they ever let down their guard? I thought maybe I should join organizations to find new friendships, but for some reason, I'm not that guy. Fraternity, you say? The thought of having to be recruited did not appeal to me. If you want to be friends one-on-one outside the bounds of a structured organization, I'm your guy, but no strings attached. Besides, I knew myself well. No way I would put up with the hazing that went on during initiation. I knew I had too much of my father in me. Looking back, I needed to get away to explore who I was as an individual. College helped me crystalize who I really was.

The only class I found helpful over my fifty-four hours of credits was my General Business class, which was an introduction to business geared towards corporations and the business world. Aced it! Highest grade in my class. Piece of cake. Interesting. In my opinion, all it did was reaffirm my feelings that college was way too many years and that they should let students get straight to their major. But that's just me.

While at Stephen F. Austin, I went to a tiny, unimpressive electronics store to have an 8-track player installed in my GTO. In a counter sat about forty 8-tracks. Looking at all those tapes profoundly touched me. At the time, I didn't realize it was a precursor to my future. Looking back, I suspect it was the spark.

"Hey Hey, Mama"
— Led Zeppelin

Riding around town in my car later that year, I became engrossed with *Led Zeppelin IV*. The album featured "Stairway to Heaven." I couldn't get enough of it. I thought it was the most beautiful arrangement I ever heard and still believe so to this day. If you never had an 8-track player, you probably don't realize that there was no fast forward or the ability to skip to any song you want. Songs reside in four quadrants, so at least you could get close. But if the piece you liked wasn't the first one on any of the four, you had to listen to other songs first. So that kept me from listening to "Stairway to Heaven" too much, which might have burned me out. That's if it's even possible to OD on "Stairway to Heaven." I suspect it's not.

It wasn't necessarily the lyrics that got me. I'm not typically a lyrics guy, although I like the lyrics to this song. It was the melody, slowly building to a powerful finale, electric guitars ablaze and the vocal octaves climbing the stairway with Jimmy Page as only he can do. In my opinion, there are very few songs with profound lyrics, and if they do, the music often isn't that great. I view vocals not as words, but rather as the singer's voice acting as an instrument. I suppose Bob Dylan ranks at the top, but I don't like his whiny voice. I suppose Jim Morrison of the Doors has some good lyrics, but I get so captured in his voice it's hard to concentrate on his lyrics. I suppose Johnny Cash's "Ragged Old Flag," and no doubt "Cat's in the Cradle" by Harry Chapin would be examples of song lyrics that move me.

When I spent my week listening to the Sirius Radio '50s

channel to see how many songs I could still remember, I was astonished. It also gave me a chance to revisit the style of that day. It hit me that there were no Fender amps or electric guitars back then. The accompaniment provided rhythmic support but very little else. No guitarist or drummer rolled into a power-packed solo. It was up to the melody and singer's voice, along with lyrics, to carry the day. And it did! It's fascinating the way they pulled that off. And if there was a period that I may have gotten into the lyrics more than others, it was the '50s. I began to realize for the first time how significant an impact the Fender amp made on music, launching a whole new era of music.

"One Fine Day"
– The Chiffons

It was the last day of the fourth semester of college. I was eager to get back home so I snuck out of my last class early. There was a backroad from Kingsville to the Bluff that I often took to be out in the country. The road was two lanes, and there were two sets of significant curves about a mile apart. The embankments dropped down low due to the terrain. I was raring to let my GTO out, but about a quarter mile back was a highway patrol car within my sight. Tapping my fingers on the wheel as I approached the first curve, I had made up my mind. As the first curve started it's descent I stepped on the accelerator, hugging the road at the fastest speed I could go. As I came out of the curve, I let the Goat eat. I needed to get into the second set of curves before the highway patrol came out of the first. I was not a daredevil by nature, and I never did anything against the law other than get into races when challenged. As I approached the second curve, I realized that if the trooper saw me in the distance and put two and two together he could radio for someone to head me off as I approached Corpus Christi. It was too late to turn back now. It was several more miles down the highway before I was finally comfortable in the idea that he wasn't coming after me. Let the summer begin.

I decided to celebrate by splurging on a couple of 8-tracks. The only place in Corpus Christi to get a good selection was a Woolco's Department Store. I have no recollection of what I purchased that day, although I vividly remember sitting in my Goat in the parking lot. I thought back to that tiny electronics store in Nacogdoches, and the small display of forty tapes. In Kingsville, I shopped at Durham's Electronics and Music. It was better, but not by a lot. Woolco had a pretty good selection, but come on, it was a department store. In August of 1969, Woodstock set the music industry ablaze. My friends were getting into music more than ever. I had heard about a hip music store in Austin, Texas, called Inner Sanctum Records and assumed one day Corpus Christi would get one — but why not me? I would have a head start and a reputation built by then. That was the moment I realized what I wanted to do with the next step of my life. Now I just needed to figure out how to make it happen.

I worked on my parents for about a week, explaining what the opportunity was and that I wanted to open a record store in the Padre Staples Mall. It was ground zero for shopping in Corpus Christi. They knew it meant a lot to me because the last time I was this determined was in sixth grade when I put up a fit about a used and dented cornet they were going to buy me for band class. They finally gave in and bought me a brand new one (to this day, I feel terrible about that because at the time, it was a lot of money for them). I quit the band in seventh grade when I realized I had to play football and then dress to go up in the stands with other horn players for the eighth grade game. It was a waste of money, and I would have gladly taken the old, dented cornet if I had it to do all over again. But I guess they probably got half their money back selling it to another student the next year.

At the end of the week, we came to an agreement. My dad would back me by putting up the land I filled as collateral for a loan if I transferred (once again) to Corpus Christi's college. I wasn't excited about the college part, but I needed to go along if I wanted the record shop.

I was disappointed when the mall manager, Mr. Wakefield, turned me down. He was an older man with a charming personality. I could tell he took a liking to me like a grandfather to a grandson, but there was currently a small store with exclusive rights to the music in the mall. I went down to the store to see what had subverted my plans, only to find a dark, dingy store full of posters, paraphernalia, and black lights. They had a small section of records and a few assorted 8-tracks. Surely, I was being punished for that cornet years ago. It was back to the drawing board.

Firmly believing that somewhere around the mall was the place to be, I began to look for retail space, but none was available. So my father rented the old Schockley and Easterling used car lot. We built a small, boutique-looking building with charcoal-stained wood exterior walls, and a red roof. Dad was smart enough to build it on pilings so if things didn't work out, we could haul it off and either sell it or use it somewhere else. The only drawback was that we had to run a sewage line across a vacant lot from the Exxon gas station on the corner of Staples and Padre Island Drive. We hired my good friend Buddy Seeds' dad, one of my teachers in sixth grade, and Buddy was his helper. I remember being so excited that I jumped in and helped them dig the ditch while asking for no pay. I remember jokingly asking Bob Seeds why he had been hard on me in his class, and he told me it was because he knew I had a lot more potential than I was putting out.

Dad took out a loan for twenty thousand dollars. Ten thousand went into the building. I still remember the builder firing up a big cigar to celebrate its completion. Five thousand went on a sewer line, a sign, and fixtures. I had five thousand left for records and 8-track tapes.

Today, we have a world of digital entertainment. Video games, movie streaming, iPhones, computers, you name it. When I opened Craig's House of Music, the entire entertainment industry consisted of long-playing albums (LPs) and archaic 8-track tapes for your car. But as strange as this must seem to our younger generations, it was everything we could have hoped or dreamed. *We baby boomers still look upon the '70s as that golden era of music!*

"When the Show Begins"
— Sammy Hagar

It was 10:00 AM CST on September 14, 1972. The day Craig's House of Music was to open for business. The night before, when my friend Orlando Martinez and I were riding around the Bluff, he asked me, "Aren't you nervous? What would you do if the store isn't successful?" The thought was foreign to me.

I contemplated it briefly before saying "I'll move on to something else." Or just maybe I was the risk taker that outran the highway patrol.

I was only twenty years old, and I had no wife and kids or any other financial commitments. Yes, my dad had some collateral on the line, but we could resell the building, and I could have a closeout sale to recoup most of my $5,000 in records and tapes. There would be some sunk costs, but I could get a job and help my dad repay the loan. I decided only to take a salary of $400 per month, and I still had money saved up from my summer job the year before. And there was also the adage: *nothing ventured, nothing gained.*

The retail business requires merchandising to highlight your product and an attractive store design to look appealing. I believed that the album covers would be the marketing in my store. Thousands of dollars are spent on the cover design by the record labels, so why not capitalize on their investment? I designed a wooden bracket built with a lip so the albums could face forward on the wall. I lined the entire back wall of the store, five rows high, to display the newest releases.

Making do with a small store, I designed a single fixture to hold the catalog albums. The much smaller 8-tracks needed to be secured, but I still wanted the customer to control the tape in their hand. I had my custom fixture maker, Julian Alvarez, build a large case with plexiglass that could lock. We cut round holes in the plexiglass, big enough for a customer's hand yet too small to extract the 8-tracks.

As will be demonstrated later, I have always been a big believer in inventory control. It would be best to have enough of each item so as to not run out, but not so many that you tie up the dollars that you could use to purchase more inventory. Working on a tight budget made it all the more critical. I kept a close eye on the better-selling albums and wrote down the slower-selling catalog items to reorder.

In 1972, there were no computers. The Commodore 64 8-bit home computer didn't come out until 1982. I had a landline, one of my dad's used NCR cash registers, and an adding machine. Cell phones didn't exist, nor did fax machines. To place your order, you called an order taker at HW Daily, the wholesaler in Houston that I used, and they had to write it down. The cash register had a crank that would open the drawer if the electricity went out, but I thought it was so cool I never plugged it in. I used it as a secure cash box, and I would tally the receipts at the end of the day to know how much money I took in.

I didn't attempt to select my initial inventory. A limited budget gives little room for error, so I told HW Daily to choose wisely for me and that I had $5,000 to spend. I drove to Houston the next day and picked up my order.

I learned customer service from my mom in the Dairy Queen.

She was always polite and attentive. They understood that she cared about them. I wanted to make sure my customers were happy with their purchases. Having a small stereo system in the store, I opened one of each new album. When a customer asked me how good I thought an album was, I reached for an open copy and said, "Why don't you hear for yourself?" Over time my regulars knew to ask on their own. Corpus Christi had a small population of Black people that lived on the other side of town. For many of them, purchasing an album was a significant investment. Over time, the word got out that I would let them listen to the latest releases: Kool and the Gang, Smokey Robinson, the Temptations, and Marvin Gaye, just to name a few.

And I put what I had learned from my dad to good use: integrity, commitment, fiscal conservatism, and always pay your bills on time. In a way, I had been in business school since I was fourteen years old, working in the family business. Watching my parents run their Dairy Queen taught me the basics — even how to count change back from my old NCR, which is a lost art these days.

"Hooked on a Feeling"
– Blue Swede

Customers showed up from day one, but not en masse. After running radio ads and getting the word out in the best ways I could, I had enough revenue to afford loan payments, my salary, and restocking my inventory. Reality set in. This was going to be a process, but at the time, becoming wealthy was not the important thing.

The important thing was that I no longer had to take classes that I didn't enjoy (yep, I convinced my parents I needed to concentrate on the store and would maybe attend college the next year). I graded myself based on how well my store performed, instead of someone grading me. I loved visiting with my regulars and got to know them on a personal level. Although not a musician (short of blowing a few notes in sixth grade on my cornet), I had an excellent ear for what would be a hit. An example is Aerosmith's first album, *Aerosmith*, released on January 25, 1973. In March of 1974, they released their second album titled *Get Your Wings*. The leading rock radio station in Corpus Christi, KZFM, began playing a song released from the second album. I was perplexed. How could a second album be released without releasing "Dream On" from the first album? Yes, it was different and took a few times listening to it to bring out its mastery, but this had to be a big mistake. But several months later, KZFM began playing "Dream On." It's one of the only times I can remember where a single broke from a previously released album.

I used that talent to my advantage over my years in the record business. Customers relied on me to level with them on which new albums were worth buying, and I even learned each customer's taste in music. One day a regular came into the store and said, "I'm headed over to the mall to do some shopping and don't have much time. Just pick me out three albums you think I will like and I will pick them up when I'm done." That also shows you how badly the mall needed a good record shop.

Sales were growing on a predictable path. I was having a lot of fun in the record business and still had time to be a twenty-something, enjoying the nightlife with friends. I wasn't getting wealthy, but I never thought about hanging it up.

"Hit Me With Your Best Shot"
— Pat Benatar

I didn't do much shopping at malls, but I did have a craving for a Chick-fil-A. It was on the corridor that the creepy little record store was, so I thought it would be good to check in on how they were doing. To my shock and dismay, there stood Durham's Music, the same store I had shopped at in Kingsville while attending college. Ninety percent of the store was cheap stereos, car stereos, and accessories. Only one long rack of albums and a few 8-tracks separated them from a pure electronics store. I stood dumbfounded, feeling like someone had punched me in my gut.

Sitting on the bench outside, watching customers going in and out while eating my chicken sandwich, I decided to approach the mall manager again. Surely that little rack of records didn't qualify for exclusive rights in the mall. That just made no sense. The always affable Mr. Wakefield apologized profusely, but reaffirmed Durham's exclusive rights to music sales in the mall. He said his hands were tied. Crazy as it seems, I still liked the guy.

Not one to let negativity absorb me, I decided to make the most of things. Since my store name was Craig's House of Music, I would add Craig's Car Stereos, which were a hot commodity in those days. Some people even thought that the car stereo company owned the store. My first employee was Brenda Seeds, Buddy Seeds' wife. I only needed someone four hours a day so I could get out, eat, and run errands. Brenda eventually landed a full-time job. David Solar was one of my regulars, and when I told him I had lost Brenda, he stood there with a big grin on his face and said he would like to take her job. David was attending college, and it would help him with living expenses, so I hired him. David did some car stereo installations, which helped sell more car stereos and allowed David to make a little extra money — a win-win.

Still in my early twenties and unattached, I took advantage of the nightlife. It helped me pass the time and keep my mind off of the missed opportunity to open a store in the mall. I had taken on a roommate, Jerry Boucher, who was at Flour Bluff High my senior year. Jerry, a deputy constable, was an affable sort and a good copilot when frequenting the Electric Eel, the local disco club. If you had asked Jerry, I was his copilot, and he probably would have been correct. Jerry passed away several years back, but I can still vividly see his face now. At the time, the song "I Shot the Sheriff" by Eric Clapton was a big hit. Every time they played it at the club, he would wait for the line "I shot the sheriff" and wave his finger back and forth as he sang along "but I didn't shoot the deputy" with a big grin.

The apartment we shared was new, clean, and reasonable. I look back today and find it hard to believe the apartment only cost us $200 a month, *all bills paid*. All bills paid might not compute with anyone younger than fifty these days. One would have to imagine electricity was not that expensive back then. It probably had to do with living in South Texas, an oil and gas state, with an oil refinery ten miles away.

I might be biased, but the years 1968 through about 1982 were the grandest era for music. Fifty years later, two of Sirius Radio's top channels are *Classic Vinyl* and *Classic Rewind*, along with *Deep Tracks* for the real diehards. Television commercials quite regularly use '70s music in the background. The last time I attended a hockey game in Saint Louis, that's all they played.

Here are a few strange but interesting memories I have of working in Craig's House of Music during the early years.

• • •

My dad liked to go to auctions. He had purchased an old, run down, '50s Cadillac in the '60s, which was parked outside the garage. Salt air had added a nice layer of rust. I got a phone call at the store; Debbie Harry was in town for her concert, and she had read an ad in the newspaper about an Elvis Presley Cadillac for sale. Debbie had a good friend that owned several of Elvis's old Cadillacs and called me by his name in a questioning tone. I assured the lady she had the wrong number. She told me she was adamant the number she called was in the ad.

It took a while to sort things out in my head, but then I laughed. My dad must have placed the ad. I explained to Debbie that it was most likely my dad's dilapidated Cadillac, and assured her Elvis had NOT owned the car. But I did not sort things out fast enough to ask her for backstage passes before she hung up. I was left feeling like she wasn't actually interested in the Cadillac but instead in talking to her old friend.

• • •

A customer of mine was in the store with a friend. His companion was one of those guys that liked to talk — and brag. He told me his uncle was Dean Martin. For those of you too young to know, Martin was a singer, movie actor, and part of the Rat Pack of Frank Sinatra, Sammy Davis, Jr., and Joey Bishop. I smiled and said, "That's great."

He said, "No, I'm serious."

I smiled again and said, "I believe you."

Then he asked "Can I use your phone?" and proceeded to make a phone call. He talked to a man for a second and then handed me the phone, saying it's my Uncle Dean. I had a short conversation with a man who sounded old and maybe a little intoxicated. To this day, I have no idea if I was talking with the real Dean-o.

• • •

There was the kid that said his stepdad was Tommy Lee Jones and that Tommy was a mean son of a bitch. This kid was goofy and a little unpredictable — the kind you want to get away from in a bar. I can't say that I believed him, but I didn't doubt the stepdad may have had probable cause. Years later, at a San Antonio Spurs game, I saw Tommy Lee Jones in the stands. I learned he had a ranch outside San Antonio. Maybe the kid had been telling the truth.

• • •

I participated in a golf tournament put on by a record label. The match was at the Pedernales Country Club southwest of Austin, Texas. Our record representative told us Willie Nelson owned the club and had his recording studio there, but he would not be a part of the tournament. I just assumed he was *on the road again*. The course was pretty much a goat track, but I had fun nonetheless — plenty of beer and fun people. When the round was over, I couldn't wait to relieve myself. I stood at the urinal, doing my business, and someone came out of a back door and took the one next to me.

"How you hittin' em?" the man said in a familiar voice.

"Not that good, Willie, but I'm having a great time!!" I replied.

• • •

One day, a charming kid came into my store. Probably as nice of a guy I had ever met. It was evident from the way he handled himself that he was a cut above. He paid with a check, which was unusual for someone fresh out of high school. After he left, I looked at the name on the check. *Stephen Butt*. No wonder, Stephen was the son of Howard E. Butt, Jr., and great-grandson of Florence Butt, founder of the largest and best-run supermarket chain in South Texas in the year 1905. The H-E-B Grocery Company was headquartered in Corpus Christi, Texas at the time.

Little did I know it was a precursor of things to come.

"Break on Through
to the Other Side"
– The Doors

One morning, I got to work and the phone rang. It was Mr. Wakefield from Padre Staples Mall. Gleefully, he apprised me that Durham's Music, after a year and a half of operations, was pulling the plug and leaving. I waited anxiously for his following words. He told me I could rent half of Durham's space and that he had committed the other half to someone else. Without hesitating, I replied, "I'll take it!" I didn't even think to ask him how much the rent was, but there was no chance it would have scared me off.

It had been around three and a half years since I first tried to rent a space in the mall, and now the time had come. I had weathered the storm. My small store's early yearly sales started at $69,000 and had now grown to $125,000, a modest gain over those three years. The long wait finally paid off, and it was time to shift into another gear. After the mall built a demising wall to separate Durham's music into two spaces, I laid out the store on a piece of graph paper. It was twenty by eighty feet — only 1,600 square feet total — but it was three times the size of my first store. And, I was finally in Padre Staples Mall.

There wasn't enough space for record bins in the middle of the store, so I built them on the entire right wall, the back wall, and part way back up on the left wall. Still believing the new release jacket covers should be fully displayed, I placed several rows above the bins to showcase the latest hits. I then built shelving along the left wall from the front of the store to where the record bins met up. I ran a counter in front of the

8-tracks on the wall that housed the newer tapes. The top was made out of plexiglas with the same holes to let customers handle the tapes. My employees stood behind the counter, pulling tapes for them off the back wall and answering any questions they might have had. We built a small counter on the front left side of the store for a cash register, leaving access to the tapes. By now, I had upgraded to a newer (but still used) machine. To enhance the customer experience, I bought a quality power amp — Marantz, I believe, for those of you who remember — and two pairs of Bose 901s. The 901s hung from the ceiling and had speakers on the back instead of the front to enhance the ambiance. Boy, did they. The sound in the store was phenomenal, and the best part was that the employees and I got to enjoy it.

For years, I had to watch potential customers parking in the massive lot surrounding the mall exit and disappear inside the Padre Staples Mall. Now, they would be walking past my store. I was fortunate to have a terrific team of new recruits. It was an eclectic group that gelled as a team. And of course, my trusted employee, David Solar, came with me from the old store. Bob Hamilton and I met when he was working at Sterling Electronics, where I often picked up accessories for the store. He later started frequenting Craig's House of Music, and we became friends. Bob-o, as we called him, was lighthearted, and I knew he had good customer service skills from shopping at Sterling's. Bob had been a bulldozer driver for his father's business in the small town of Beeville, Texas, so I knew he wasn't afraid of hard work. Al Gonzalez worked at another store in the mall but would visit us every day on his breaks. Al had a perpetual smile on his face, lifting the mood of everyone around him. He was not only versed in knowledge of record artists but had an interest in stereo equipment like Bob.

J.R. Elliott came to us from the west coast. He had an interesting take on things, especially for us small-town boys. Can't say it made me want to change my own take on things, but it was fun to hear a different way of thinking. J.R. was the spoon that stirred the pot and kept things interesting, as I would learn to my chagrin. On the weekends, the store would fill up, sometimes so full that customers had to wait in the hall to get in. J.R. would take out his rubber chicken and cluck out loud as he threw it into the crowded store, usually getting screams out of the female patrons. At first, I watched the aftermath closely to see if any customers were irritated, but they never were. People laughed and enjoyed the caper, resulting in the customers interacting with one another. Who knew that kind of stunt would have been good for business?

I had an interview the following week with Mary Bocanegra, a beautiful dark-haired girl. She was the quintessential definition of voluptuous. I checked out Mary's demeanor nonetheless to ensure she was a good fit. From a skills standpoint, all she needed to do was stand behind the counter, hand customers tapes, smile, and converse with them. I'm sure it turned our male customers into regulars. I probably should have paid Mary on commission.

Almost everyone working for me had long black hair and a full beard, including me. We dressed in shorts, slaps, and whatever t-shirts the record label gave us. Customers often asked us if we were brothers, so J.R. made us some t-shirts. They said, "No, we are NOT brothers."

The business was booming! All we had to do was roll up the front gate in the morning, and customers would fall in. I accompanied my dad to our CPA, Marshall Pearce, who had been his accountant for years. Marshall asked me how sales were going. I knew my seasonality patterns from three years in the business and had used them to project our full year's sales. "Half a million," I said. Marshall leaned back in his chair as if to ponder. I don't think he believed me. But I did miss the mark. We only did $496,000 — four thousand dollars short of my target at year end. Marshall's son, Gary Pearce, has been my CPA to this day. First Marshal and then Gary. They have been doing the Odanovich family's tax returns for at least sixty years. They are the salt of the earth.

For anyone that hasn't worked in a mall, it is an energizing experience. Our corridor was a tight-knit community, and I became friends with store owners like John and Molly Trice and their manager, Terry Shaw. John and Molly owned the surf shop across the hall, selling surfing gear to the troves of Padre Island surf rats. Our stores were a good draw for one another. Or the Kimchinani brothers, who owned The House of India just down the corridor. Sammy was new to America and manned his store while his brothers sold tailor made suits around the country. He was a good guy and always had a smile on his face, so I paid extra attention to him. One day, Sammy took me to his apartment. He had been slow cooking a pot of something all day and the pungent smell hit me as I walked through the door. "Come on Craig!" I remember hearing him say. "I made this special just for you!" He placed a piece of bread on my plate and then ladled the vegetables on top. That's when I fell in love with curry.

The following are a couple of fond memories of this period.

• • •

Typically, once a day, I would take a break to clear my head. I'd just walk around the mall, contemplating, and sometimes getting a full head flush by operating the Pong arcade game just on the other side of Chick-fil-A. It helped being blessed with good reaction time, like having something slip from my hand and catching it before it hit the floor. Pong was a popular arcade game in the early '70s. I used it every other day to decompress, and, as a result, I became pretty good at Pong. But there was a sweeper that had mastered Pong, and while he would often get challenged to a contest, he never lost. Having depleted the competition, he went out looking for a challenger, eventually winding up at our store. The sweeper said he had noticed me playing and wanted to challenge me. When I hesitated, J.R. egged me on. Word got out, and before long, a pretty good-sized crowd gathered around us. It took me a bit to get over my nerves, and I fell behind early, but I became more and more focused and locked in as the game moved along.

As I steadied myself, the puck began to move faster. It felt surreal, similar to the time I took my GTO out on a small country road that was seldom used and decided to find out what the top end was. I can remember the 400 cubic inch engine winding up every step of the way. When I reached the 120 MPH mark — the last number on the speedometer — it continued to accelerate until I had pegged zero. Telephone poles zipped by like they were only twenty yards apart. And then I realized I'd better take it down because not only could the engine blow, but if a farmer with a load of hay pulled onto the road, I was a goner. But it wasn't that easy. A car moving at that speed (possibly 140 MPH, but it's impossible to know) takes time to come back down. The process was slow, arduous, and agonizing — somewhat of an out-of-body experience. I swore to myself that if I made it out of this alive, I would never, never do this again. And I never did.

The Pong puck was exploding off our perfectly placed paddles, so much faster than the telephone poles zipped past in my GTO. But this time, I only had the downside of losing, not dying, and by then, it had become a matter of pride. I don't remember much after that, but I do remember walking away victorious and drained. The sweeper hounded me for a rematch, but quite frankly, I had no desire to go through that again. I would just hang onto his crown. And I have to this very day.

• • •

Throughout your life, there are specific albums that define your journey. The album *Equinox*, by the rock band STYX, was one of those. They were pretty much an unknown band at the time, but when we opened up a copy, we all knew this was something special. One night we even stayed in the store after closing hours, pulled down the see-through metal gate, sat around the floor, and cranked up the stereo. The sound from the 901s exploded off the walls. I'm sure workers could hear the music in the far reaches of the mall, but we didn't care. The mall was closed, and the customers were gone.

Shortly after STYX came to town as a headliner for Wishbone Ash, it was inevitable we would attend the concert. The crowd knew little about STYX unless they had been one of our customers we turned onto the group. They put on a phenomenal show! Better than we had even hoped for. Fortunately for us, I had decided to load up on their album and 8-track. We were probably the only place in town that had copies after the first hour of the next day. But unfortunately for Wishbone Ash, a band that plays soft melodies, they paled in comparison. Corpus Christi was notoriously a rock-n-roll town. The Wishbone boys were probably mad at the promoter for pairing them with STYX as a wall of people left the auditorium partway through their performance. We were leading the exodus. Later, around 1980, Iron Maiden took their maiden voyage to Corpus Christi. They were relatively unknown at the time but no doubt a big hit with the crowd. I mean, KZFM radio's tagline was "THE ROCK OF THE BAY!" After the concert, I couldn't keep their debut album in stock until I finally placed a massive order. The Capital Records rep told me on one of his visits that we were selling more Iron Maiden out of our store than any store was selling in any city in America — New York and Los Angeles included.

"More Than a Feeling"
— Boston

Success is a funny thing. You get a bounce in your step, and suddenly getting out of bed in the morning becomes effortless. It has a way of making you want more. I started by increasing my advertising to boost sales. Define your value proposition and promote your product. Then, determine what is the most cost-effective way to send the message. In the '70s, the leading advertising avenues were newspaper, radio, and television. If you had a mega sale, you placed a full-page ad in the *Caller-Times*. For radio, you did KZFM for rock and KEYS for more commercial bubble-gum groups. And if you wanted to build your brand, you used television.

The marketing moves satisfied my yearning for growth through the Christmas season, but then what next? Bob had sales experience, was a guitar player, and had an in-depth knowledge of stereo equipment. There was an open space next to the record store, so we rented it. Several months passed as we built out the space and negotiated for territory rights with top stereo brands. Like getting into the mall, a small outfit had the rights for Boise in Corpus Christi, and it took a while before we could add it to our lineup. Before too long, we opened Craig's Sound Gallery! Those of you old enough to have been around in the '70s may have owned one of these stereo system components. Name brand companies like Marantz, Bose, Pioneer, Sherwood, Advent, Infinity — any of them sound familiar?

In 1976, I signed a lease to expand into a mall in Victoria, Texas, about ninety miles up the road. In doing so, I took on a partner. As you recall, Greg Smith grew up with me in Flour Bluff, riding out the hurricane. Anyone that knew Greg would not have guessed he was from a well-to-do family, as Greg had no pretense and carried no air about him. I can't remember a time in high school when he came to our house wearing shoes. But he had a serious business mind that kept us working together on and off through the years.

An interesting fact: Greg's great-granddad, Burton Dunn, at one time owned the entirety of Padre Island and drove his cattle through Laguna Madre to graze in the summer months. Back at the turn of the century, there was no barge channel to contend with. Greg is fond of telling the story of the time his granddad got caught on Padre Island during a hurricane. Back then, there were no cellphones to warn him of the impending danger, and I suppose no radar to even know it was coming. Burton rode out a hurricane on top of the highest dune with a coyote and a rattlesnake as companions. As the story goes, while the hurricane was roaring, the three amigos were so distracted by survival from the storm, they left each other alone. When it was over, they all went their separate ways.

I sent my longest-tenured employee, David Solar, to run the Victoria store, which we also called The Sound Gallery. Dave did a great job, and the store, although not nearly as high volume as Craig's in the Padre Staple Mall, was very profitable. The success whetted our appetites to expand once more. Greg and I set out to find another mall location.

Ridgmar Mall in Fort Worth, Texas, was a newly-opened mall that did not have a record store. Had we been able to find a mall location, say, in San Antonio or Austin, we wouldn't have opened a store so far away from home. But as luck would have it, there were no sites available.

Dreaming big and thinking we would continue to expand, we decided to open a small industrial space in Irving, Texas, as a distribution center. Greg traveled to Fort Worth and hired Jeff Fandrich, who moved from Meeker, CO to help him build the store. I focused on opening direct accounts with the record labels, allowing us to purchase records and tapes at lower prices. By combining the orders for all three stores, we had the volume to buy box lot quantities, which lowered our costs further.

Greg hired a college friend he had met while attending the University of Texas to design the store. Greg's stint in college wasn't any longer than mine had been, and he had left to run his father's concrete plant about the same time I opened my first record store. But his contact came in handy with a favorable price, and the design was classy. The only issue they encountered was when they found themselves surrounded by a large contingent of union workers. One of the union guys picked up Jeff's electric saw and slung it across the room to get their attention and let them know he meant business. And that's the day we found out Greg and Jeff needed to get a union card. That never would have happened in Corpus Christi, but we weren't in Kansas anymore, so we had to continue following the yellow brick road.

By the time they had our Ridgmar store up and running, I had the distribution center ready to go. From that point on, the three record stores placed a weekly order with our distribution center. Dallas was a regional distribution hub for the surrounding four states. The prominent record labels like Warner Brothers and Columbia had distribution centers right down the street. That allowed us to pull records and tapes from stock previously bought in box lots and place new orders from the labels in time to receive and check in new products by Thursday. On Friday morning, one of us would run the van full of merchandise to the three stores. The only problem with this plan was that we needed to keep expanding to fully maximize the profitability of our distribution center. And that was the original plan. Greg named the distribution center Tsunami — the reference being that we were going to grow and roll over the competition. I guess we were young and feeling it! A combination of early success and testosterone.

Our Fort Worth store was not as profitable as the other two, to our dismay. It was the best-looking store of the three, but unfortunately, the Ridgmar Mall was on the outskirts of Fort Worth and had trouble getting traction. Then a series of events happened. Both Corpus Christi and Victoria announced modern, new malls. The new malls would devastate our Victoria store as the current mall was very outdated. And although the Padre Staples Mall would survive, the sales volume would take a hit.

Mine and Greg's first response was to approach the new malls for space and build new stores. But that wasn't to be. Both malls had already committed to national chains that had the first right of refusal to any new malls the developer built. Greg and I sat down for a strategy session. In our conclusion, the new malls had outflanked us on two fronts. It was time to rethink our strategy.

"I'll Give You Money, I'll Give You Lovin'"
— Peter Frampton

I remember waking up in my girlfriend's bed to the most exhilarating song I had heard in a long time. I had no doubt it would be a huge success. Dressing rapidly, I drove straight to work. I looked into how many copies of Peter Frampton's new live album I had on order. If the rest of the songs on the album could hold serve, the album would be a monster. The next thing that caught my eye was that it cost me little more than a single album even though it was a double album. The market was charging more than a single album but not as much as a double. *Frampton Comes Alive!* was going to bring in monster profits!

The record label typically gave you an extra ten percent off on pre-orders. There was still time to up my order and get the discount, so I did in a big way. My margin just got bigger. Months later, the album was a bigger success than was hoped for by me or the label. They decided to offer another ten percent discount and gave us an extra thirty days to pay. It was time to back up the truck again! Kooter Roberson, an ex DJ and Record Factory worker that followed me to Fort Worth, went with me to greet the freight truck. We stood with our mouths open when the freight truck dropped off an entire pallet of albums to the distribution center. And we wound up selling them all.

"We Will Rock You"
– Queen

Greg and I rented a two-level apartment in Irving, Texas near our warehouse. One weekend, some friends from Flour Bluff came to stay at the apartment before a Cowboys/Vikings playoff game. Of course, everyone was a Cowboys fan except me. I had become a Minnesota Twins fan while spending a summer in Minnesota with my grandparents, aunt, and uncle in 1961. It was the Twin's first year in Minnesota, and I was little league age. My cousin, Kevin West, who was my age, and I played little league baseball in town and would listen to the Twins on an old radio with our uncle. The Cowboys had come into the NFL in 1960 and the Vikings in 1961. Living in Texas, it was a tough choice at first, but the Vikings eventually won out.

The night before the game, I had gone to bed early, but the others stayed up late into the morning, drinking. The morning of the game, I was rip roaring to go. But the others were sound asleep on the floor. I stepped over Kooter Robertson, pulled out a Queen album, placed it on the turntable, and cranked it up. "WE WILL, WE WILL ROCK YOU" boomed from the Infinity Q1 tower speakers. The drinkers were not amused, but it did the trick.

Frigid north wind swirled around the stadium. We were too cold to drink beer and too dumb to have brought whiskey flasks. Early in the game, we noticed a commotion in a section close to us. Someone had brought a bunsen burner to the game and it caught their snowsuit on fire. And all we could think about was how nice it would have been to warm our hands on him. I can honestly say I have never been colder. My only other memory was two of the guys standing in the back of the van holding Kooter by his pants while he peed out the open back doors. But I digress.

"Ah, Breaker One-Nine,
This Here's the Rubber Duck"
— C.W. McCall

Citizen Band radios were a big deal in late 1978. You might remember some lingo from television shows. *Hey there, good buddy... 10-4, roger that... Smokey, the Bear....* There was a demand for more channels, so the manufacturers and the Federal Communications Commission worked on a compromise. The manufacturers were allowed to go from twenty-three channels to forty. The catch was, the manufacturers had to stop selling twenty-three-channel CB radios by the end of the year, and it was already the fall. As with any upcoming model update, the consumer slows their buying of the old model and waits for the new. Anyone that has purchased a car is aware of the end of the year late model sales. The manufacturers' problem became our opportunity.

James Ewing was our salesman from an electronics company, Wholesale Communications, which was run by Sumner Bowen. Sumner stepped out on a limb and purchased truckloads of CB radios from the manufacturer, Clarion, who was dumping at super low prices. Remember, if they didn't sell by January 1, 1979, they would have to use them as a landfill. Sumner instructed James to get them out to retailers as fast as possible, somewhat in a panic. Wholesale Communications did not distribute in Fort Worth, so James talked us into taking a boatload of them to sell in our Ridgmar Mall store. It was more inventory than Greg and I felt comfortable with, so James said we could return any we didn't sell.

Clarion co-oped a full-page ad in the Fort Worth newspaper. The following day, there was a line of people waiting to get in.

The line was out the front door all day. We let James know, and they loaded up another truck of radios and sent them our way. When the dust settled, we made out like Smokey the Bandit.

"Leaving on a Jet Plane"
— Peter, Paul and Mary

Walking into a large Peaches Record Shop in Fort Worth the day after seeing the opening of *Star Wars* at a local theatre, I stood in the middle of the store in awe. White knotty pine on the walls, as well as pine record bins. It blew me away every bit as much as *Star Wars* had. At that moment, I knew what I needed to do. It was time to regroup.

I sat down again with Greg and explained I needed to protect my home turf in Corpus Christi with a Peaches type store. Having been outflanked in Victoria, Texas, we realized our Tsunami was in danger of turning into a Bob Hall Pier surfing wave. We agreed we should put the Fort Worth store on the market. With the new mall coming to Victoria, we would ride out our lease. A month before the lease expired, we would hold an everything-must-go sale.

I honestly can't remember how Bill Durham, of Durham's Music in Kingsville, Texas found out we were selling the Fort Worth store. I do remember Bill flying us up on a plane he had leased. My instincts told me Bill was a bit wounded when I took over his failed store in Padre Staples Mall and made it wildly successful. I imagine he was enamored with the thought of buying our store in Fort Worth. After touring the store and looking at its financials, we boarded the plane to go home. Bill is one of those guys that has an air about him. Not someone I would welcome as a close friend. He came from money. I could say Bill had an aristocracy complex. Greg sensed the same.

Once we were airborne, Bill offered us hard liquor, but Greg never drinks, and I would never drink during a negotiation. Bill poured himself a large bourbon anyway. After his first drink, he made his move. Bill said he would pay what we were asking for the Fort Worth store, but only if we sold him the more profitable Victoria store. Did he not know about the new mall coming to Victoria? We asked Bill to visit the pilot, which he had previously done, so Greg and I could confer.

I'm not overly proud of what we decided, but Bill was, after all, playing hardball. He would leverage the Fort Worth store to acquire both. We called Bill back and said we would sell him the Victoria store if we came to terms. We offered favorable terms, so he accepted, pouring himself another large glass of bourbon to celebrate his crafty deal.

Plan A was complete. Now it was time for me to turn to Plan B: fortify Corpus Christi. I soon found out Greg gave his newly married sister, Linda, his take to use as a large down payment on a new home. I would use mine to build out a new big box record store in Corpus Christi.

"Rock the Casbah"
– The Clash

Returning to Corpus Christi full-time, I went in search of a suitable location. The store needed to be around ten thousand square feet with reasonably priced rent. I felt the perfect place was a space on the corner of South Padre Island Drive and Weber Road, so I submitted a bid. When it was turned down, I found out the landlord somehow was told we closed the mall location at night, sat around listening to music, and smoked pot. Was it about the night we sat around after work and listened to the STYX album? The only night we had ever done that? I would never know. The funny thing is that if I had been the landlord, I would have done the same. Yes, we had long hair and beards, but when it came to business, I was all business. I had rules. Never date an employee, and never get intoxicated on the job.

Not to be deterred, I went on the hunt for a location again. And this time I struck paydirt. The site was everything I wanted, and the rent was cheap. Twenty-five cents a square foot. I did, however, have to do all of the finish-out on my dime. But this meant I got to use the knotty white pine I had wanted all along. Teaming up with my fixture man, Julian, we began the process of bringing the store together. I hired my high school friend, John Visosky's father, to build out the premises.

"Blinded by the Light"
— Manfred Mann's Earth Band

I split my days between the new store buildout and my record shop in the Padre Staples Mall. One day, a woman and her daughter came into the store and stood there looking around. The daughter had the most beautiful face and a vulnerability about her. She looked over all the hairy employees as if intimidated. The combination was irresistible. But what if she leaves and I never see her again? The solution came in the form of her sister, Tricia, who happened to be an employee. Tricia was an exemplary employee and looked like a cute version of Little Orphan Annie. Tricia's mother and her sister, Cathie, were there to see how Tricia was getting along.

A group of us were going out that night to the top club in Corpus Christi, Granddaddies. I asked Tricia to tell her sister she was welcome to come along, which she did. I sat next to Cathie the whole night. Years later, Cathie said she didn't remember that. One thing led to another (a song by The Fix), and we went on a date. Not knowing anything about the newly released movie *Midnight Express*, Cathie dug her fingernails into my hand all night. Not the best start, but a start nonetheless. Those of you from Corpus Christi might remember the two other clubs we all frequented: Cooper's Alley and Cantina Santa Fe.

I visited my new megastore to find that progress was moving along splendidly. The store was looking spectacular! The tongue and grooved, knotty white pine-lined walls were warm and friendly, rising twenty-five feet to the ceiling. The left side of the store had a one-hundred-foot-long counter that separated the customers from the one-hundred-feet of open storage to house the thousands of cassette tapes. Since I was big on customer service, employees would roam the space behind the counter, hand the cassettes to the customers and answer any questions. It provided the one-on-one interaction I desired. My employees were accessible to all. If a customer needed help finding an album in the dozens of wooden record bins on the floor, they could ask for assistance. The employees had explicit instructions not to point in the direction of the album and say, "over there." Instead, they would walk with the customer and hand the album to them. There is nothing more frustrating than asking for help and still not finding what you were looking for.

The control center was a large, hexagon-shaped platform, built out of wood in the back of the store. It rose above the record fixtures. Customers walked around the hexagon-shaped counter to access employees who were using the interior space to check newly-received albums into our inventory books. In those days, large stores like ours got a promotional copy marked "NOT FOR SALE." If we didn't get one, we opened a new copy anyway. If a customer wanted to know what the new album sounded like, an employee would place it on the high-fidelity turntable. The four pairs of Bose 901s driven by twin sister, shiny black, Amber power amplifiers filled the large facility with concert-quality sound. The platform would soon provide a staging area for high-profile rock bands to sign autographs and converse with hundreds of customers. The setup offered controlled access, so the artists retained their physical privacy and enough counter space for all band members to interact with fans simultaneously.

The walls in the back of the store had ten-foot-high mirrors, giving the feeling that the store was twice the size. On the middle mirrors, an artist painted the store's soon-to-be-iconic logo: *Craig's Record Factory!* Complete with smoke billowing up from the logo's factory. Once again, I relied on an old high-school buddy. Roy Smith, who I once gave the privilege of being the first to ride in my GTO.

Customers walked up a ramp in the front of the store onto a wood floored platform to check out, walking past accessories to purchase if they so wished. The newly-released albums were on full display by the hundreds before they walked up the ramp. In later years, they were greeted at the cash register by none other than my mom, who, like at the old Dairy Queen, got to know all of them. She was our rock-n-roll gramma.

Fueled by a barrage of radio ads and a full-page ad on the back page section of the *Caller-Times*, the grand opening was a roaring success. Corpus Christi music lovers flooded through the front door, mouths wide open as they roamed the vast music playground and took in the sights and sounds. There was little talking — just a lot of gawking.

"Changing of the Guards"
— Bob Dylan

David Solar, my trusted employee, returned from Victoria after we sold the store, and he helped us out at the Record Factory. Bob, J.R. and Al were off to other opportunities. But this opened the door for another cast of characters to emerge. They were fun-loving, yet more reserved. Two of them were my girlfriend, Cathie's, sisters, Tricia and Nancy. Nancy was as cute as a bug and underage so I made sure the guys looked out for her. My good friend from my basketball days, Orlando Martinez, came on to handle the bookkeeping. My father showed up every morning after picking up the money from the mall location. He added it to the Record Factory receipts to deposit in the bank. My parents had worked hard in their Dairy Queen, and the new store allowed them to move on from the grind, which pleased me. Liz James became one of my favorites. In the business, the record labels let you send back any defective records along with a percentage of albums that didn't sell. The job was tedious, as the paperwork was different for each label. All clerical. Most employees shied away from returns, but not Liz. She would tackle mounds of boxes with a smile.

Months after I opened, the owner of Ashley's High Speed and Boogie Record Store, Ashley Johnson, approached me about selling his store. The Record Factory had put a dent in his store sales. Ashley was an actual record aficionado, who had worked at the infamous Inner Sanctum Records in Austin. Ashley later became one of the premier dealers of vinyl records after the days of analog technology were no more. He worked in the basement of his Victorian style home in, I believe, Joplin, Missouri, selling vinyl all over the world. I liked Ashley and respected his knowledge. From a business standpoint, I knew he had a small but loyal following, so I offered him a job and agreed to purchase his inventory at his cost. Ashley was not much for inventory control or the boredom of sending back albums that were no longer selling, so half of his stock had to be sent back as returns. Disposing of the useless inventory was not a problem. I ran a tight ship and had ample credit to return the albums to the labels.

"There is No Room for Mistakes.
We Sailing the Tight Ship For Sure"
— Stephen Marley

Now that I was purchasing a million dollars in inventory a year, I decided it was time to take my inventory control up a notch. Computers had not come on the scene in any meaningful way, so I devised a manual system. It was as simple as in-stock, sold, ordered, and received. I made a page for every album we carried. I had the sales volume to purchase directly from the labels, so I kept each label's inventory in separate books — one for Warner Brothers, one for Columbia, etc. When the product came in, we logged it into the received column. When it came time to generate orders, we added the received albums (or tapes) to the in-stock column and subtracted it from our current inventory from the previous inventory. We knew what every item sold over a specific period of time.

The inventory was purchased based on how well they sold:
  Hot new albums, we ordered weekly.
  Slower selling new albums, we ordered bi-weekly.
  Hot selling catalog titles, we ordered monthly.
  And deep catalog titles, we ordered bi-monthly.

The formula was different for each:
  Two months supply for bi-weekly catalogs was ordered every other month.
  Two months supply for hot catalogs was ordered monthly.
  One month's supply for slower-moving new releases was ordered every two weeks.
  And three weeks supply for the hot new releases was ordered weekly.

The formulas were centered around never running out of a particular album and ensuring they sold within the sixty-day period I had to pay for them. So, in essence, customers always had the album they came in for (customer satisfaction), and I had the album paid for by the time I sent the check (Craig's delight). It meant I had no capital tied up in inventory at all. A rarity in any retail business, even today.

And yet, there was an exception to the rule. Every so often, the record labels would run a promotion. They gave you a ten percent discount and 120 days to pay. I capitalized by purchasing a six-month supply, but only of the constant-selling catalog albums that I knew would continue to sell for years. Buying an extra sixty days beyond the 120-day terms was warranted. The capital cost to hold inventory is much less expensive than the ten percent discount. Besides, it would be the only capital cost of inventory I had.

But what I'm most proud of is my holiday season inventory control. Every Christmas season followed the same pattern. The week after Thanksgiving was the slowest, and each week after increased. But the last week before and after Christmas was a factor by a multiple of up to three-point six times the slowest week. It allowed us to be fully stocked the day before Christmas and when people had money given to them for Christmas the following week. It also allowed me to know how much to let the inventory level sell down going into the slower months, post Christmas.

You could come into Craig's Record Factory or Craig's House of Music ten minutes before the stores closed on Christmas Eve and were guaranteed to get your album of choice — unless for some reason the label was out of stock when we ordered.

You see, I loved music, but loved the business more. I could tell you if a record would sell, but I could not tell you the band members names. It's also why I shied away from hiring members of local bands. Their minds were on music, not business. I understood and didn't fault them, but I had a business to run.

After putting my inventory system in motion, I assigned an employee to each label to track the inventory, so that no one had to do inventory full time. Ashley Johnson could name the members in most bands and had intricate knowledge of groups that were not commercial. He was the go-to employee for serious music buffs. But I soon learned why the inventory I had purchased from his store was so out of whack. Ashley was responsible for the Columbia Record label that had as good a catalog as any other. The freight truck arrived with the order Ashley placed several days later. The boxes of records and tapes were massive, so I called Ashley to my office. I asked him if he followed the formula I had given him. Ashley replied. "Oh, I thought it would be easier just to order box lots." It took me days to calm down.

"Going to the Chapel"
— The Dixie Cups

Cathie and I had been dating for over a year. She was the first long-term girlfriend I ever had. Our values aligned, and we got along well. I was sharing an apartment with my friend, Jerry Chancellor. He was an engineer working for a gas plant. We were both making good money, so he suggested we build a house to have an asset instead of paying rent. At the time, being a businessman, I thought it was a good idea.

Cathie and I were having dinner at Howard's Barbeque. I can't remember what she was having, but I was very much enjoying my plate of beef ribs. As I ate my ribs, I could tell Cathie's demeanor was markedly different. I had never seen her like this and knew something was bothering her. It was a wake-up call.

The ribs began to lose their flavor as I pondered the situation. It didn't take long for me to figure out it must have to do with buying a house with Jerry. Then it hit me that she may have been thinking about marriage and that would throw a monkey wrench in our relationship. I was on the verge of losing her.

Although I was twenty-seven years old, I had honestly never given marriage a thought at any time in my past. I have to admit, Craig's Record Factory took center stage. But now, I knew it was time to set that aside and ponder a fundamental question: if I don't ask Cathie to marry me, how would I feel the rest of my life if I lost her?

I've always been one to assess a situation, trust my instincts, come to a decision, and take full responsibility for that decision. I picked up my last juicy rib and then laid it down. Cathie seemed lost in thought as she played with her food. I said, "Cathie, let's get married!"

Cathie looked up with a smile on her face and replied, "Yes, let's do it!" Now I was in uncharted waters. Unprepared, having never watched Hallmark Channel movies. What now!?

Cathie took control. "Can I go shopping for an engagement ring?"

"Ah, all right," I replied, feeling guilty I hadn't already brought one to the rib dinner, but then, how could I have?

"How much can I spend?" Cathie shot back. Totally out of my league and ill-prepared to answer, I leaned back, and in this instance, I made too quick of an uninformed decision. I'm a generalist, versed in an extensive range of topics — politics, sports, world affairs, history, religion... you name it. But the inner workings of marriage? I was less than an amateur.

"Let's see," I thought. "How much to spend?" I thought this whole engagement ring wedding thing was a bit much. I mean, why would you waste a lot of money on an engagement ring when you had to turn right around and buy a lovely wedding ring. "Three hundred dollars," I said. And off to the mall, Cathie went.

Cathie called me from a jewelry store, informing me there were no rings that inexpensive. I opened up about how I was not too fond of the idea of putting a lot of money on an engagement ring and would instead put it in a wedding ring. "Silly," she replied. "An engagement ring is the wedding ring!" Geeze, I thought, who knew?

Now I had to figure out how much to pay. I had become friends with the jeweler next to the Sound Gallery in Victoria. It didn't matter that I no longer owned the store. I took Cathie on a pleasant drive the following Saturday and let her choose an expensive ring with a big discount. Hey, that's what any businessman worth his salt would do, right?

After a beautiful outdoor garden wedding, almost pulling out in front of a car on the way home, and a wonderful vacation in Hawaii that my parents paid for as our wedding present, we began to settle in. We just celebrated our forty-first wedding anniversary, so love is all that matters.

My sisters, Cherry and Jan, reminded me how I told them at the age of nine that I would NEVER get married. I had written it in a sealed letter that they could hold. My parents told me they knew I was serious when Cathie was the only girl I had ever brought to meet them. Sometimes in life, you are the last to know.

"I'm Taking What They Are Giving 'Cause I'm Working for a Living"
— Huey Lewis and the News

Was I working for a living? Hardly! If God created the perfect job, it would be working at Craig's Record Factory. I would sleep in until 9:00 AM, put on a t-shirt, slaps, and shorts, and let my *hair freak fly*. I'd listen to the latest music with my working friends on a concert-quality sound system while visiting with my customers.

Having top artists come to the Factory to sign autographs was something special. We had hundreds of fans/customers surrounding the perfectly designed podium, all while blasting out the band's best songs. And all before they headed out to go to the concert. The following are some of the more memorable events.

• • •

Def Leppard was on their first tour to America to promote their newly-released album, *High 'n Dry*, in 1981. They ranged in ages from eighteen to twenty-two. The UK-based band turned out to be the nicest kids, looking as if they were in awe of the states. I imagine Texas was somewhat of a culture shock.

• • •

Judas Priest was the opposite. A better-known band, Craig's Record Factory, was packed to capacity. But the band did not show up on time and gave us no information on when they might get there. After half an hour, the tension mounted. It was more excitement than disappointment. After an hour, the crowd became restless, and I both felt bad for them and was worried they might leave. I'm a very punctual person by nature because I hate to waste someone's valuable time. I'm more likely to arrive early. If someone had called, letting me know they were running late, I could have apprised the audience. I'm also pretty easygoing, but minute by minute, my temperature began to rise. Finally, they arrived, and I began to cool down. Until I realized they were oblivious to the situation and pretty much acted like jerks. My dad's DNA kicked in, like the time he went after the Bandido leader in the Dairy Queen parking lot.

I stepped back for a second to gather myself. I began to realize that action on my part might jeopardize the autograph signing session, so I chose to get into my car and drive away. Sometimes that's the better part of valor. Besides, it would have gotten me in hot water with the record label. After an hour, I returned, and all was well.

• • •

The boys were back in town. We didn't have an autograph session, but the label invited me to meet the band the morning after their concert. I walked into the conference room at the hotel and looked around. Thin Lizzy band members were crumpled together in a corner, half asleep, looking like hell. Feeling half sorry and half put off, I turned around and walked out. I never thought of it as any big deal.

• • •

I pulled up to the downtown Sheraton Hotel in a limo provided by Epic Records. They wanted me to escort Ted

Nugent to the autograph signing. Having just gone through the Judas Priest fiasco, I thought it an excellent idea.

I went up to his second-floor room and knocked. Out came a man with cat scratch fever, wild as the animals he now hunts with a bow. The limo drove down scenic Ocean Drive on our way to the Record Factory. Halfway there, Ted realized the crazy act did not affect me, so he switched to an average person. From that point on, we developed a good relationship and discussed many interesting things. But once through the back door, he flipped a switch, and he was back to Ted, the entertainer.

My customers loved him, as well as my employees. Ted was highly approachable and let fans and employees take all the pictures with him they liked. When the session was over, Ted walked over and put his arm around my shoulder. "Hey Craig, will you do me a favor?" Ted asked. "If I can," I replied.

Ted then asked me to tell Denise Mora and her friend, Lilly Villarreal, that he would let them backstage at the concert. Denise was exotic pretty, with long, silky, black hair and a dark complexion. I do not know her nationality, but wouldn't be surprised to find out she had American Indian genes. The following day, I realized he wanted to get into those jeans because Denise wound up going on the rest of the tour with Ted. I was happy for them, but I wished Denise had at least called me to say she was quitting. Thank goodness Lilly came back and told me. If I ever see Ted again, I've got a lighthearted bone to pick with him.

• • •

Along with being in the business, I was given free tickets to most concerts. I went to Led Zeppelin, Doobie Brothers,

and many more. My only disappointment was the The —
guess — Who concert. Burton Cummings quit the band
moments before they flew down from Canada. So *these eyes*
never got the opportunity to see him.

"She's Got a Ticket to Ride, But She Don't Care"
— The Beatles

Along with having autograph signings with bands, we also sold most of the concert tickets in Corpus Christi. At first, I balked, not liking the service charge. I felt my customers would think I was gouging them, but after realizing that they had to pay the service charge whether we sold them or not, I fortunately came to my senses. Selling thousands of tickets brought people to my stores, both Craig's Record Factory and Craig's House of Music in the mall, and with the people came increased sales.

One day, I realized we had a new Bayfront Auditorium that held 2,600 people, with plush seats and impeccable acoustics. I saw the opening and started calling bands. The first band was Christopher Cross, shortly after he released his single hit, "Sailing." It was the biggest audience he had played for at the time. A few months later, I called his manager and asked if I could bring him back to the Memorial Coliseum, the larger venue where Ted Nugent had played. By now, Cross was red hot, and his manager rudely told me not a chance. A year later, Cross's manager called me after his career crashed and asked if I still wanted to bring him back to Memorial Coliseum. I turned him down and said that ship had sailed.

Next, I brought Stevie Ray Vaughn to the Bayfront Auditorium. Cathie's aunt, Shirley, was in town with her sons. To this day, Shirley tells the story of how Stevie autographed the front of her white t-shirt. One report was that he kissed Shirley's hand and cheek. Stevie was pretty sweaty. Although Shirley will tell you it grossed her out, there is no arguing it left a lasting impression.

Stevie rocked the Bayfront like no other before or since. I felt like the Memorex guy sitting in his easy chair with wind-blown hair.

"The Stuff that Dreams are Made Of"
— *The Maltese Falcon*

One day in around 1980, I ordered a couple of VHS and Betamax movies from Warner Brothers. I could see the potential of selling movies in this format, but not at the listed price. Who was going to buy movies for $79.95? The films sat on the shelf, collecting dust, until one day, a Naval officer from the Naval Base in Kingsville bought one. But after a few days, he brought it back, claiming it was defective. Suspicious, I played it in a VHS player, and nothing was wrong with the tape. The airman was adamant about getting his money back. I wouldn't say I liked his tone, and I very well could have refused, but I realized what was going on. After watching the movie one or two times, he realized it wasn't worth the price he paid. Since I agreed, I gave him his money back and stopped thinking about video movies.

Several months later, the Warner Brothers rep came in from Austin. He said, "Did you know some stores are renting movies in Austin?" I asked if it was legal. He said it wasn't. When he left, I sat down in my office and pondered the concept. I had already known the studios wouldn't get anywhere selling movies at such an atrocious price. I felt the studios would eventually come around to realize this as well. And finally, if the studios didn't want us to rent videos, they could stop selling them to us. Figuring their sales would plummet if they cut off the rental business, I gave that an almost zero chance of happening. Studios had a dilemma on their hands.

Unfortunately, we didn't get clarity for several years. Similar to what is happening in cryptocurrencies now, the government takes in a lot of taxes from the product, but they won't draft regulations. Then they claim the market isn't safe because it's unregulated. Studios were doing the same thing back then. Ninety percent of their home movies division's revenues were coming from movie rental stores, but they sued anyway. It was tied up in courts for years before a judge's first-sale doctrine ruling. The first-sale doctrine stated that once a studio sold their product, they had lost control of it. I often wonder, what would have happened if the studios had prevailed?

So what to do? Corpus Christi was off the beaten track. Surely the studios would go after retailers in the metro areas first. And if the studios won in court, the worst they could do is put a stop to renting. By that time, I would have made a handsome profit, and I could sell off my inventory.

There was a section of the store that was perfect to house the videos. As I mentioned earlier, customers walked up a ramp and turned left to check out and walk out of the store. The ramp sat in the middle, so there was ample space to the right. I built a counter in front of them where we housed the movies, similarly to the cassette tapes. We then used the walls to display the movie posters. It was like a store within the store.

During the early days in the video rental industry, not only did you purchase the new releases, but they were constantly making catalog titles available. In later days, you bought thousands of catalog titles to open a new store. But there weren't thousands of titles in the beginning. I imagine production facilities were going up rapidly to speed up the release of older movies.

Business boomed! The shelves got fuller and fuller with movies of all kinds. Craig's Record Factory dominated video rental the same way we dominated records and tapes. At the time, I believe we charged five dollars a tape for two-day rentals. Then I began to realize how lucrative the rental business was compared to selling records and tapes. When we sold an album or video, we kept thirty-three percent of what we took in. But the asset left the building forever, never to sell it again. With video rentals, we took in the money. But after a few days, the movie asset came back to be rented again and again.

"There's No Place Like Home"
— *The Wizard of Oz*

I was moving into a new phase of my life. Cathie gave birth to our two beautiful children, eighteen months apart. Jack West was first and Michelle Brooks the second. We had more responsibility, so I became more serious about business. No more leaving work to go to the nightclubs. After a while, Cathie resumed her college studies in education, so I either stayed home with our kids, or my mother and father watched them. Not that we didn't have fun, but we were more apt to have fun at Cathie's parents. Her father, Cactus Jack, was a hoot. C.J. always kept things lively, while her mother, Bet, was the perfect hostess. Before we were married, I would often eat at Cathie's parents' house. Her mother was an excellent cook. I guess I just assumed Cathie would be as well.

Wanting to keep the business momentum going, I began going to the Consumer Electronics Shows (CES). The summer show was in Chicago, and the winter show was in Las Vegas. You can probably guess which one I preferred. After one show, we began selling Coleco and Attari video games. True to form, I built displays with TV sets so our customers could test out the new games. The most significant break was at the January 1982 Vegas show. We were about to leave, when David Solar said I needed to see what he had stumbled across.

It was a company named Porta Video. They had wrapped a smaller version of a VHS recorder in a blue, molded, hard case with a built in handle. The marketing was good, as six of them stacked in a small display. In early 1982, VCR penetration must have been around four percent, but you could get to the other ninety-six percent if you rented them a VCR. Porta Video operated like a franchise. Purchasing the Nueces County territory, where Corpus Christi resided, I told the salesman I would test the concept in Craig's Record Factory. If they proved themselves, I would commit to the Rio Grande Valley.

A territory required the purchase of sixty machines. That was a $60,000 outlay. More than I was comfortable spending for a test, but my instincts told me it would work. And it did. Renting a machine with two movies for $19.95 a night, we had them all rented out each weekend. The move added an average of $4,000 of revenue to video sales a week. The concept was to do a revenue-sharing program with other retailers. We would provide the rental machines and movies; They used their labor to rent them out. They kept thirty percent with no investment, and we retained seventy percent. I figured the more store traffic, the more rentals. The obvious thing was to make out a list of potential retailers and rank them. At the top of my list was the dominant supermarket chain in central and south Texas, H-E-B (which stood for Howard E. Butt, the founder and grandfather of the impressive young man that wrote checks at my original store).

Fortunately for me, H-E-B headquarters were located in Corpus Christi. So, armed with a Porta Video, several videos, and new slacks, I walked into my first meeting. The general merchandise buyer behind the desk greeted me warmly. He listened patiently to my spiel and then said he would make another meeting with the new manager coming in to replace him. He was an older gentleman and didn't seem to know Craig's Record Factory when I mentioned where I was from, so I felt maybe it was for the best. Neither pleased nor disappointed, I patiently waited for my next meeting.

Several days later, I went hat-in-hand to meet the new purchasing manager with a Porta Video and a couple of movies. Roger Davidson, a strapping man with a pleasant demeanor, sat behind the desk. Roger was close to my age and had transitioned from store operations to the purchasing department. He was also staying in a hotel until his wife, Debra, could move down to Corpus Christi with him. We launched into a discussion of our movie preferences, which was an encouraging start, but the whole concept of watching movies at home was foreign to him. Handing him the video recorder and tape, I encouraged Roger to sample the product in his hotel room. The video machine was a hit and enabled Roger to pass the time until his family arrived. After Roger watched his two movies, he brought them back to Craig's Record Factory and rented more.

Having a background in operations, Roger reached out to the regional operations manager, Gus Kroos. Gus asked his store managers if any of them would allow us to conduct a test. As luck would have it, Tom Short, the store manager of the Kingsville store, was relocated from the Corpus Christi area and was an avid movie renter at Craig's Record Factory. Bill Durham, the man that purchased my record stores in Fort Worth and Victoria, had not caught onto the new opportunity. The new mall had come to Victoria and rendered Craig's Sound Gallery obsolete. By then, he had closed his store in Fort Worth as well. The poor guy seemed always to be a day late and a dollar short.

I soon found out that East Texas Periodicals already had videos in dozens of H-E-B stores. I'm not sure Roger had known about this either, as he was new to his job. The

Flour Bluff H-E-B was one of their stores, so I drove over to investigate. It took a while to find their movies, but I eventually discovered a single floor display. The display had around one hundred films locked behind plexiglass.

East Texas Periodicals policy demanded the customer purchase with a credit card. The customer was charged the total cost of the movie if not returned by a designated time, and they could not rent more than two movies at a time. I felt this policy was rooted in distrust of their customer. Renting video machines was not a part of the program, reducing their target audience to only four percent of the general population who owned a video recorder. It's as if their movies were made of gold, and they were Fort Knox. Later on, I realized that because they were a magazine and book distributor, they had no concept of retailing. Their reps restocked magazine racks. H-E-B paid for the inventory, and if stolen, H-E-B bore the brunt. Trusting customers was never a part of their business model. They were out of their league.

My policy would remain as it was at Craig's Record Factory. All the customers had to do was show a driver's license. They could choose to pay with a credit card, but we accepted cash and checks as well. We had two years of experience in the video rental business and knew that far less than one percent of our customers didn't return their movies. We trusted our customers, and we trusted H-E-B customers. Why would you limit yourself to those who only had credit cards? In the early 1980s, most people didn't use credit cards like they do today. The other advantage was renting Porta Videos, opening the rental experience to all.

The Kingsville manager of H-E-B gave us an end cap on the freezer aisle in front of the check-out counters. I couldn't have asked for a better location to promote our business. We had one shot to impress, so I had Julian build a six-foot counter. The counter had plexiglass on the front to display movie jackets, drawers to house the films, and racks of Porta Videos behind the counter. Our employees stood between the counter in front of the video machines and used the countertop to transact the purchases. We had receipts with two carbons for copies. When we settled up with H-E-B once a week, we brought back a copy of the receipt and left a copy for H-E-B.

At this stage of my business, I began to attract college students. The first was my sister-in-law's boyfriend, Robert Najera, who had just graduated from the University of Texas. The second, Rick Muliix, who was still attending college and worked full time in the summers. My time was being spent more and more with the new endeavor, so Robert became manager of Craig's Record Factory. I needed someone professional looking to man the counter at Kingsville, so I selected Rick. Both were clean-cut, attractive, courteous, and had excellent people skills.

The opening weekend in Kingsville, I operated the booth with Rick. We placed a TV set on top of the kiosk, and Rick chose *Rocky* to demo. During the fight scenes, husbands left their wives and surrounded the screen. When the fight scene ended, we looked at them and asked, "How would you like to watch a video in your own home?" Their looks were those of bewilderment. It took us showing them how to hook up a Porta Video to the TV for them to understand. Their confusion soon turned to smiles as they pulled out their wallets. That weekend, Rick and I rented all sixty VCRs with an average of at least two movies per machine. I'm sure the revenue numbers blew H-E-B management away!

"I Feel the Need —
the Need for Speed!"
— *Top Gun*

The order came down from Roger to gear up for expansion. The Corpus Christi area was to be first. And after, I would take the show on the road to the Rio Grande Valley. Endcaps in H-E-B stores were valuable space. Manufacturers paid large sums to expose their brands, which I didn't have. The solution turned out to be moving the video department into the spacious general merchandise areas. But where? Space was hard to come by there as well, but at least I didn't have to pay for it. I was responsible for the fixtures, and I decided to bear the cost of customizing them to fit the space offered up. I brought graph paper and a measuring tape to each future store. Movie inventories were housed behind the long counters, so each storage unit was fit to size. Movie jackets were placed on shelving custom-built on the merchandise floor for customers to browse. We placed the actual movie tape in a hard plastic casing to protect it when the customer took the movie home. I helped with suggestions on where they would best fit but decided to cooperate as best I could. It was a chance to make a first impression, and I didn't want to screw it up.

The rollout went smoothly, and by Christmas, the best time to rent videos, most of the Corpus Christi H-E-B stores were operating. I convinced Roger that the best strategy was to let me open the highest volume H-E-B's first. This way, I could generate more capital for expansion. He understood that it was in the best interest of both me and H-E-B. I also convinced him that opening low-volume stores would be a poor allocation of capital, and again, Roger agreed. Looking back, I shudder to think what might have happened if Roger hadn't happened onto the scene. Providence was on my side.

"The Day the Music Died"
— Don McLean

Christmas sales were strong, and we geared up for the Rio Grande Valley expansion in 1983. By now, I needed people to service the stores. Our sales rep visited their stores each week, meeting with general merchandise managers. They tallied the sales slips and generated a billing invoice for the manager to sign and send to accounts payable. While there, our reps picked up any defective inventory and dropped off the new releases.

By now, it was apparent that this was a separate operation from Craig's Record Factory. As such, I set up an independent corporation: Odanovision Inc. I gave ten percent of the shares to my parents, two-point five percent to David Solar, Robert Najera, Orlando Martinez, and one percent to my in-laws.

Around this time, John Marmaduke, the president of Hastings Music, sent his top lieutenant to inquire about purchasing Craig's Record Factory. Hastings ran large entertainment stores in mid-sized markets. By now, every decent-sized market in the state of Texas was dominated by either Sound Warehouse, Peaches, or Hastings Entertainment — except in Corpus Christi. As much as I enjoyed the music business, I realized I was being tugged in the direction of building out H-E-B. Besides, I could use both the capital from the sale and the single focus of my new business opportunity. And I needed my best employees working on H-E-B with me.

I offered Hastings what I felt was a very fair price for the sale of Craig's Record Factory, but they turned me down. A good customer, Ben Blanco, heard about it and told his friend, Richard Powers. Richard owned a small record distribution company out of San Antonio. He wanted Craig's Record Factory as much for increasing his record distribution as his retail sales. He was burning the candle at each end. Richard didn't have the money to purchase the store outright, so I took twenty-five percent down and let him pay out the rest over three years, which he did.

I should have known it was time to leave the record business when one day I overheard two teenage girls talking while I was stocking some records in the bins. "Did you know Paul McCarthy was in a band before Wings?" one said. "No way!" the other replied.

With more working capital and a steady inflow of cash from the sale, I rented an office/warehouse on the outskirts of Corpus Christi. The top floor was offices and the bottom a warehouse. My office looked out over a large grain field, which I very much enjoyed. And the warehouse gave us the staging area for inventory needed to expand and the growing number of new release videos we required to service the growing number of stores.

"Elementary, My Dear Watson"
— *The Adventures of Sherlock Holmes*

One day I was deep in contemplation as I looked out over the waving fields of grain. That's when it dawned on me that videos were a commodity. And as commodities, each video had its own unique value. The industry was renting all movies for the same price. The going rate by then was three dollars a night. I now viewed it as counterintuitive. Why should we charge the same amount for catalog movies as new releases? Like an automobile, the car's value decreases the moment you drive it off the car lot. I decided to split up movies into three categories: new releases, hot titles (which were older but still popular), and the older catalog movies. New releases were expensive, so three dollars was warranted. But hot titles and catalog movies were already paid for. I sent out a directive that we would implement the three/two/one system. Three dollars for new releases, two dollars for hot titles, and one dollar for catalog titles.

The change was an instant success. We dramatically increased the number of movies we rented, along with increased revenue. I learned later on that although H-E-B enjoyed the higher margin on video rentals, they loved the fact that customers had to return them. The average trips to a grocery store were between two and three times a week, and video rentals helped move the needle.

"Surley, You Can't be Serious"
— *Airplane*

The Rio Grande Valley was a huge success! Roger Davidson opened up San Antonio and Austin to me. Each market had more potential than all the stores we had opened before. BUT, it would take a lot of capital. I had a very good relationship with the Corpus Christi National Bank. CCNB is the bank that loaned me the money to build out Craig's Record Factory, and we had repaid that loan ahead of schedule. It's also where we deposited our growing amounts of money. At that time, Craig's Record Factory had deposited $1,400,000 a year, the store in the Padre Staples Mall deposited $600,000 a year, and Odanovishion was on a run rate of $4,000,000 a year. Albums and cassettes sold for an average of six dollars each in early 1984. So, at today's rates, revenue from the two record stores would equal around $6,000,000 a year.

I had an excellent relationship with my banker. She was young and sharp. I didn't think borrowing a couple hundred thousand would be an issue, but the decision was not up to her. Someone in the bank thought video rentals was a fad, just like the early round of video games. The only thing they had in common was the word 'video.' An SBA loan would have taken a lot of the risk out of it for the bank, so they required we go that route. But SBA loans were time-consuming and cumbersome.

The loan came through in the nick of time. I never let H-E-B know there was an issue because I didn't want them to think I was too small of a company to build out their stores. And in fact, I did build out San Antonio and Austin. It helped that the price of VCR machines had come down substantially, as all new electronics do.

We had an outstanding December sales season, but in January providence played a hand again. Both San Antonio and Austin pretty much came to a standstill when south Texas had a historic snowstorm. For ten straight days, all of our VCRs and movies were rented. Cashflow shot through the roof. And so did the banker that forced me to go the SBA route. My father had taken the fact that the bank made us jump through hoops as an insult. So every week, he prepaid a chunk of the SBA loan. By the time spring came, the entire loan was retired.

The bank took me out for lunch to celebrate. My banker and most of the participants were thrilled for me — everyone except the bank officer who spent weeks filling out the paperwork. I could have boasted, but I chose not to make eye contact with him. Watching him eat in a gloomy mood was enough. I liked the man on a personal level, so I felt sorry for him.

"Fasten Your Seatbelts!
It's Going to be a Bumpy Ride!"
— *All About Eve*

Roger Davidson and his boss, Pat Dewayne (a fan of Odanovison), discontinued East Texas Periodicals' expansion into H-E-B stores. I find it hard to believe ETP remained stubborn and never adopted our strategy. But they decided not to remove them from existing stores. I assumed it was because they distributed magazines to H-E-B and did not want to sour the relationship. I understood this line of thinking. I asked Roger if he would approve my flying to Houston to purchase their stores. Once I got the green light, I scheduled a meeting with their president.

Knowing they were a corporation and wanting them to take me seriously, I broke down and wore a suit. I also went out and purchased a faux leather briefcase that was attractive. Briefcase in hand, I entered the building with their president, Ken Stillings. I'm sure no one had told him the nature of the meeting, but that became clear soon enough. Ken was short and balding. Maybe twice my age. He was also one of those high-intensity guys. The kind that runs a company with an iron fist and is used to getting his way.

He sat there listening to my presentation and offer to purchase his stores, reading the consternation as I went along. I wrapped up and sat back, hoping to negotiate. In no way did I expect what came next. Mr. Stillings lashed out. "What gives you the nerve to come in here with an offer?!" he began. "Don't you realize who we are!? We should be buying YOU OUT." It went downhill from there. A good, old-fashioned tongue lashing. I kept my cool, but since I didn't get the answer I hoped for and he had made it crystal clear that I wouldn't, I took my leave.

It was a blessing in disguise. You know, that providence thing again. It wasn't two months until H-E-B informed me that they were intrigued by the video rental business and wanted to buy me out. And that was the end of East Texas Periodicals' video rental program in H-E-B.

"Show Me the Money!"
— *Jerry Maguire*

The thought of H-E-B wanting to be in the video business themselves never entered my mind. But when they did, I was not surprised. Maybe it was the Mercedes I had purchased. It was only the five series, but who knows. I didn't buy it as a status symbol. I bought it because the first car I learned to drive was an old 190D series. The 190D was rounded like the original Volkswagons and slow as molasses. The top speed was eighty-five miles an hour. My dad used to take me with him to see his parents in Minnesota over the Thanksgiving holiday once I was old enough to share the driving. It was a twenty-five-hour drive from Corpus Christi to the iron ore range in Minnesota, where my dad's dad had worked as an immigrant.

To make it up and back in four days, we drove non-stop each way. The roads were two lanes back then, and when we had to pass a car, we would drop back, then build up speed and time our move around the vehicle in front of us. Looking back now, the Mercedes didn't play a role. They could see how much they were paying me and how lucrative the business was. And the fact they could infuse more money into the departments and increase the number of times customers would enter their stores to return the movies.

H-E-B could have asked me to pull my movies and leave, but that would have required re-equipping the stores with VCRs and videos. Instead, they offered to purchase my business. The offer was three times our cash flow and amounted to a little over $2,000,000. I thought about making a counteroffer but decided against it because they had offered to purchase the company instead of removing my product. I had put all my eggs in one basket, and this was the consequence. I had no one to blame but myself. But the $2,000,000 took the sting out of it.

An officer of the company asked me to come to finalize the transaction when he would be in Houston on business. Cathie came with me to the meeting. I remember she was embarrassed by me for sipping my hot coffee and making a slurping sound. Although we were executing the contract that day, H-E-B did not want to take over control for a month. Since I was still going to operate the stores, I convinced him to purchase my new releases over that period. The move put another $200,000 in my pocket.

During the negotiations, H-E-B never mentioned its full intentions. Not knowing my future or the future of my employees, I picked up the phone and called David Cook in Dallas to inquire about the Blockbuster franchise. It was early 1986, and David built his first Blockbuster in 1985. I would have been getting in on the ground floor. But after we closed, Pat Dewane, the Vice President of General Merchandise for H-E-B, called, saying he wanted me and my whole team to come work for H-E-B. Pat asked me what I was paying myself. Due to our success, I had just boosted my salary to $120,000 a year. Pat said that was more than some VPs in the company made. I remained silent on the phone. Pat agreed to my salary demands. Little did I know I was once again putting my future into the hands of H-E-B.

My parents netted $200,000. Orlando Martinez used his proceeds to purchase rental properties in and around the small town of Aransas Pass. Orlando built a small empire in Aransas Pass over time. He stayed on for seven more years, servicing the H-E-B stores in and around Corpus Christi. This increased his capital flow for more rental houses.

Robert Najera netted more because he purchased some of David Solar's stock. David had his eyes on an expensive big screen TV. My in-laws netted $20,000. C.J. had an excellent job at the Reynolds Aluminum Plant, but putting four daughters through college took its toll. They could get out of credit card debt purgatory with the money, which made me feel good.

"Louis, I Think this is Going to be the Beginning of a Beautiful Friendship"
— *Casablanca*

In 1987, we all packed our bags and moved to San Antonio, Texas. H-E-B set up a separate Video Division outside their corporate framework to give us autonomy. My title was General Manager, which was unique to their conventional titles of Directors and VPs. And they gave me carte blanche of the day-to-day video rental operation.

The real reason they purchased Odanovion became more apparent when they instructed me to expand the video departments in the forty largest stores. They planned to wall off a portion of the general merchandise departments. The stores would operate under our guidance, but the employees would still work for the individual stores. We would be responsible for stocking the stores and managing their movie inventory.

The result was equivalent to adding nuclear weapons to a tugboat. The departments, which we referred to as 'rail cars' due to their long, skinny shape, could house upwards of four thousand VHS tapes. A literal video store within a store. Four thousand tapes were enough to carry all of the top renting catalog tapes. And they could do between $400,000 – $500,000 in revenue annually.

It was a massive project to process all of the VHS tapes, so we leased a warehouse and filled it with racks for processing the videos. I created a position for product and distribution. I convinced my old friend and business partner, Greg Smith, to join me. This move paid off handsomely down the road, but that's later on in the book. The move also gave me someone to strategize with who thought the way I did.

Around that time, Blockbuster approached H-E-B. They wanted to rent a space in an abandoned store five miles from our warehouse. It got H-E-B thinking all the way up to Fully Clingman, the President. H-E-B had just moved into their epic new offices just off the San Antonio River, on the south side of downtown San Antonio. The land was an old arsenal in early Texas history. The architecture was stone, very classical looking. They even kept the old stone arsenal with its approximately eight foot thick stone walls. But the fact that their headquarters had been in Corpus Christi meant that they were all familiar with Craig's Record Factory.

So the story goes, someone in upper management said, "Hey, Craig had a big entertainment store, why don't we have him build H-E-B a video superstore?"

When asked if I thought I could put one together, I replied, "Sure! When would you like it?" I was not expecting the response to be six months, but I went about my business undaunted. That is until I got my first taste of how corporations operated.

Some brilliant soul decided it would be a good idea to form a committee. I cringed at the thought but had no idea how bad it was going to be. We were to meet once a week. After the first meeting, I came out panicked. We had spent two hours and virtually accomplished nothing. I spent my whole time educating them on video rental and why most of their suggestions wouldn't work — *time to hatch a plan.*

The first thing I did was contact a fixture firm that did store layouts for free, hoping to sell fixtures. I told them they had one week to work with me on the store plan. I pieced together a presentation on everything from inventory to signage, and presented the store layout. To my shock and delight, the head of the committee said, "I think Craig has this under control. I'm not sure we need to hold these meetings in the future." So we didn't.

Word must have gotten around, because the next thing I knew I was invited to a meeting at Charles Butt's house. Charles is the most brilliant businessman and leader I have ever had the pleasure to meet. H-E-B is rated at the top or close to the top of the best companies to work for every year. And after working at H-E-B for seven years, I can attest that it's due to Charles. It's a perfect blend of taking care of and respecting his employees, yet throwing down the gauntlet when it comes to being competitive. The official word for an employee was a partner, which conveyed his respect. It was also why merging Odanovision with H-E-B was a perfect match. Our cultures were identical. H-E-B has had — and still does have — the highest market share in their territory. Many new supermarket chains learned that to their detriment when entering H-E-B's Market.

Charles' home is in the historic King Williams District and has all the character of a long-gone era. The meeting consisted of Charles, Harry Beckner (a top consultant), Fully Clingman (President), and someone new I had not met. Dennis Hatchell was hired away from a smaller grocery chain in the Carolinas, and he was a good-looking, mild mannered sort. I took to Dennis from the get-go, and our relationship flourished from there. Especially after they informed me Dennis was to be my new boss. A match made in heaven, I thought. It also didn't hurt that Dennis was new and had a lot of catching up to do with his major role in H-E-B management. I met with Dennis in his office once a month and updated him on how things were going and what the next steps would be. Dennis would chip in where he had advice. The meetings were efficient, leaving me on the right path.

As I look back, my biggest weakness may have been managing upward. It was a foreign concept to me. Even my dad left me to carve out my path. Reporting to anyone had never been a part of business for me. Hopefully, they appreciated the fact there was no need for handholding, and I never missed a deadline. Later in my tenure at H-E-B, I started putting together a recap of my Monday meeting with staff, both as a way to better inform H-E-B of our progress and a document of each department's tasks.

My business philosophy has always been to hire ambitious, self-motivated people. I am detailed in running a business, both logistically and strategically. However, I have never been a micromanager. The top of my list of attributes for a fellow employee is *follow-through*. My role was to tear down roadblocks and answer questions; If I can't trust you to follow through without me checking on your progress, you are taking up my time.

I knew that to be fair to our managers, it was my responsibility to update them on my thought process and what we needed to accomplish. Monday morning meetings were the only time we were all together, and they were the best time to communicate with partners. Discussing every manager's tasks allowed the other managers to see the overall picture. Better-informed management makes better-informed decisions without my needing to be there.

I guess it's somewhat of a teach-a-man- (or woman, as I had

a good ratio of women in management) to-fish theory. What better way to help managers grow and trust in their decision-making skills? And finally, I knew how good it felt to be left alone to do my job without someone looking over my shoulder.

It was a fast paced six months. Blockbuster caught wind of what we were doing and wanted to punish us, so they fast-tracked a store across the street. Their move caused us to go into overdrive to beat them open. We worked around the clock the last three weeks and darn near didn't get opened in time. Pat Dewane's son worked for us and reported to his father we would not open on time. The VP of Marketing put together a terrific advertising campaign with a lot of dollars behind it. Not opening would have been a total disaster, both for H-E-B and my career.

But I had been through this before when I opened Craig's Record Factory, when I had a full-page ad scheduled. I have always been a good estimator of time and had little concern we would make it. All it took was calling in a few more employees and working all night, just as I did with the record store. At six in the morning, I got home and went to bed. I did not know about the large contingency of executives about to descend on the store at opening. Or the massive crowd that was waiting to get in. I learned of this when Fully Clingman called to congratulate our team and me, waking me up.

We only had one checkout counter with two computers. Two lines of customers went all the way to the back of the store. When I got there at one o'clock, I discovered the ancient air conditioning units on top of the old grocery store had crapped out. It was a sweltering summer day, and so was our store. Customers had sweat running down their faces. It was a Saturday, and H-E-B maintenance couldn't promise they could arrive until the next day. Not acceptable, so I returned the favor and called Fully. And he fully cooperated, having a crew there in several hours. In the meantime, I took what employees I could spare and made a run to the local convenience store to stock up on cold beverages. We handed them out to our inconvenienced customers in line, waiting for their turn to check out.

Dennis Hatchell took me to dinner the next week with our wives. I introduced them to Shrimp Pizzano, my favorite dish. I relived the days leading up to the opening. Dennis told me a similar story about when he was charged with getting a store open in Denver that was running behind. Dennis got it opened in the nick of time, just as I did. He told me he had been busy on something else and wasn't thinking about the opening until riding in his car early that Saturday morning as he listened to the radio. The radio personality said, "Do you know H-E-B is opening a store today with no groceries?" Dennis said he almost swerved off the road. I also remember him calling my wife's Suburban a 'Texas Cadillac.' I use that line a lot.

Blockbuster opened two weeks after we did. A week after that, their dignitaries showed up to visit their store. We were scouting Blockbuster and knew they had very little business. I can still remember a group of six suited men walking across the busy highway and entering our store. They stood in the middle of the crowded store in awe. I left them to their misery.

The Monday after the store opened, I designed a new counter configuration to handle the volume of customers. Using an example from a H-E-B grocery store, I laid out three counters, facing from the front of the store to the back with two registers on each side. Six check-out lanes in all. We changed to this format in the all-new H-E-B Video Central stores.

We referred to them as our 'grocery-style checkout counters.' The throughput was phenomenal, which helped with our computer terminals being slow. Barry Beitz, a programmer for H-E-B's MIS (computer department), remedied this by writing a new program in short order.

One day I received a call from Ron Denny, the Executive Vice President of H-E-B Store Operations. He explained that one of his store managers, Alan Payne, had just completed a graduate course from USC and received a Food Management Certificate. It was a unique program for grocery executives, attended by business people from all over the world. Alan went there as a store manager, so it indicated where they saw Alan in the future.

I was already well acquainted with Alan and thought highly of him. Alan was the manager of the Flour Bluff H-E-B when I opened their video rental department. Alan was also very familiar with Craig's Record Factory and an avid customer. I had already been on real estate expeditions with Bill Horvath, the Vice President of the HEB real estate department. If our first video store was successful, the plan was to expand Video Central stores rapidly. I was certain Alan's knowledge of the inner workings of H-E-B's store ops would pay off handsomely.

Our explosive store opening put things into overdrive. We were not only prepping videotapes for the forty new rail cars, but we needed warehouse space large enough to handle the processing of dozens of new stand-alone video stores. Greg Smith and I encouraged H-E-B to retrofit an old grocery store on Fredericksburg Road that had been dormant for years. Greg and I always thought as if we ran our own businesses while working at H-E-B. We paid close attention to the bottom line and wanted the Video Division to be as profitable as it was feasible. *Greg could rub two nickels together until the buffalos wanted to stampede.*

We would turn a non-performing asset into a useful one. The old store, some thirty thousand square feet, if I remember correctly, was a perfect size. Ten thousand square feet went to offices and twenty thousand to the warehouse. The offices were bare-bones but spacious and clean. We had a large conference room with an exceptionally long conference table rounded at each end. It became the hub of our operations.

Greg oversaw the buildout and systems required to hold and process the massive amount of tapes rolling in weekly. Liz James, the young woman eager to process returns at Craig's Record Factory, had made her way to warehouse manager. I couldn't have been more proud of Liz. She later became the first in her family to graduate from college.

Alan was the Director of Store Operations, and Robert Najera was his top lieutenant. Alan had more pedigree, but Robert was a seasoned veteran of video rental. He could help Alan learn the business side of store ops and take the responsibility of opening the rail cars off Alan's hands.

Rick Mulinix, the young man that opened the first video department in Kingsville, was now Director of Product Management. His duties consisted of product merchandising and department development, video games, and ancillary products like candy and accessories.

David Solar, my oldest employee dating back to my first little record shop in 1972, was our movie manager/buyer. And we were buying a lot of movies. At one point, over $17,000,000 a year worth of videos.

And there were plenty of newcomers like Art Seago, Director of Loss Prevention. Art was young, intelligent, and determined — a great guy and team player who thought in black and white. Loss of product became almost nonexistent after Art took the reins. Wanda Polasek was a long time H-E-B employee in the advertising department and a Record Factory customer in Corpus Christi. And then there was Kevin Brown, a talented young comptroller.

Later we added Roger Davidson. Roger was responsible for giving me my foothold in H-E-B, and he was the internal champion of video rentals before H-E-B purchased us. Roger was the Director of Marketing and Advertising, bringing it one step closer to the operation. Up until then, Melissa Stenicka had done a good job. Still, there's nothing like having the marketing and advertising director know the business from the inside. And who better than Roger, the man responsible for H-E-B being in the video business?

And finally, there was Alan Markert, the comptroller of H-E-B. Alan was the liaison between corporate finance as well as upper management. Alan was a big supporter of ours, but one hundred percent corporate when he first came in. After hanging with us, he gradually loosened up — a bit. He was highly talented and a significant asset to Video Central. I can still remember meeting with Alan in his office when I had just come to H-E-B. He stared at me while we talked and then finally said, "I suppose since you are a separate division and it's entertainment, it's okay for you to keep your beard." Surprised by Alan's directness, I replied with my own, "Good to hear, because my wife told me if I ever shaved it off, she would divorce me, and I'm not ready to get divorced." True story on *both* accounts.

Our team was young, talented, and aggressive. The individual ages ranged from late twenties to late thirties. The team was a close-knit group. All for one and one for all, as the saying goes. To illustrate the potential, I'll update you on what they went on to accomplish after video.

Alan Payne went on to become one of the more prominent Blockbuster franchise owners, and one of his stores was the second to last Blockbuster store to close. Blockbuster corporate stores included. Alan has written a fascinating book about Blockbuster as both an insider and his comparisons on how H-E-B ran things differently. The title of Alan's book is *Blockbuster: Built to Fail*.

Greg Smith is a three-time city council member in the prime Corpus Christi district. He owns one of the only five-star RV parks in Texas, located just outside Port A on Mustang Island. Greg holds a considerable amount of land in south Texas and New Mexico.

Roger Davidson went on to be an executive in both H-E-B and other supermarket chains around the country. He now operates a consulting firm, keeping the top Wall Street firms apprised of the current state of the supermarket industry. Roger has clients all over the world and makes semi-annual trips to London. Walmart is one of his clients as well. Roger also owns and co-manages a small food distribution company, Magi Foods in San Antonio, that has had stellar growth.

Rober Najera is currently the Director of Public Affairs with H-E-B. He's a high-ranking corporate executive.

Rick Mulinix is part owner of Direct2Connect Marketing in Houston.

Art Seago went on to become President of Santikos Entertainment, the premier theater chain in San Antonio. Art now has his own consultant company to guide smaller theatre chains.

David Solar went on to write three books. He turned two of them into screenplays and is close to getting one of them made into a movie. At the time of this writing, a major star has been cast for the lead role.

Liz James went on to a managing career in H-E-B's distribution division.

Kevin Brown is a successful developer.

Wanda Polasek worked for H-E-B from an early age and remained there her whole career. With her fat retirement plan, Wanda whiles her time away traveling America and making the most beautiful crosses from native mesquite wood. Her husband, Richard, who worked in H-E-B's construction department while we built out Video Central, enjoys his time on their ranch.

Alan Markert went on to a long career with H-E-B before forming his consulting firm. I am happy to report that he is now living in Colorado, leaving his suits and ties behind. Alan has always been an avid outdoorsman and is probably shooting a rapid in the wilds of the Colorado Rockies as you read this. I wonder if he is wearing a beard...

I will always have fond memories of our original warehouse because that's when Cathie delivered our third child, Amy Linnea. My most vivid memory was all the commotion around Cathie while Amy lay crying on her chest. I'm not much for racket myself, so I picked baby Amy up, took her to the far corner of the room in my arms, and cuddled her until she stopped crying.

"I Love Waking Up in the Morning to the Smell of Napalm"
— Apocalypse Now

Let's fast forward a few years to 1990 to spare you all of the blocking and tackling. Building out forty retail rail cars inside the top supermarkets and thirty-three video superstores is a major undertaking. H-E-B's retail store planning and design unit and their construction division were operating beyond capacity. Yet, I never heard a complaint out of them.

Both the Video Central stores and the rail car businesses were booming. We had no fear of Blockbuster, and in fact, opened a Video Central across the street from a Blockbuster any chance we could get. Operations quite often sent someone incognito to assess their store traffic. Still, it wasn't until Art Seago did some dumpster diving behind Blockbuster stores that we found out for sure.

It took a few tries, but Art stumbled across their corporate store. Their district manager made the mistake of throwing out a monthly sales report. As the saying goes, one man's trash is another man's treasure. Word got back to me, and I summoned Art and the team to our war room. The excitement was palpable.

I have never heard so much hooting and hollering. After examining Blockbuster's store sales in the four-state region, we finally knew where we stood. Any store operating within H-E-B territory was getting crushed compared to those outside our area. Next, we brought in our store sales and compared the Video Centrals across the street or close to the Blockbuster stores. On average, our stores were doing sixty percent more sales volume than their stores. It was an all-out beat down!

We also experienced a few instances where Blockbuster opened across the street from an existing Video Central. Our store initially had a ten percent drop in sales, but over four months we regained the sales loss. How could this be, you ask? Here is a blow-by-blow explanation that no one outside our team has ever known. *The secret sauce*, you might say.

Wayne Huizenga purchased a majority stake in Blockbuster from David Cook. Wayne was a brilliant businessman, but NOT a nuts and bolts guy. As with Waste Management, the trash pick-up service, he grew his business rapidly by rolling up other independent waste management companies across the United States. His focus was on expansion and the price of his stock. Instead of rolling up existing video chains, he franchised store territories, while aggressively building out his store base. In many instances, Wayne would purchase the franchises, returning them to the fold.

From what I learned reading Alan Payne's book, *Blockbuster: Built to Fail*, Wayne was loyal to his old cronies. They provided his inner circle, and Wayne did not trod outside his inner circle. Ex-Waste Management executives, who had no conventional retail experience, ran the company. Sending trucks to pick up trash every week is not exactly rocket science.

David Cook, the founder, set the original pricing policies, and Wayne's team made no effort to tinker with them. The burgeoning video rental industry was in its early stages. As in all early retail industries, the competition was mom-and-pop stores. The small owners were better retailers than Blockbuster in many instances. Still, the truth was, Blockbusters could overwhelm them with brute force and deep pockets.

Cook's rental policy went like this: All videos were rented out for two days at three dollars a day. Check-in time was midnight on the second day. We never witnessed their employees scrambling to get the returned movies back onto the shelf. They must have felt it saved labor by not beefing up their staff during the busy evenings and restocking the shelves the following day when the business was slow. To a typical retailer, it made sense. To me, it did not.

As I previously mentioned, I realized early on while contemplating videos as I looked over the waving fields of grain that movies were a commodity that had different values. I firmly believed that he who could profitably provide the most availability of new releases to video renters could dominate the market. 'Profitably' was the operative word. I will get to that in a bit.

In real estate, it's *location, location, location.* I concluded that in video rental it's *new releases, new releases, new releases.* The availability of new releases trumped all. It trumped price, and it trumped the number of days rented. We rented new movies for one day at a time. Our rental price was the same as Blockbuster's: three dollars. I assume Blockbuster felt they had the upper hand because the customer could keep their movie out for two days. I felt we had the upper hand because by renting a film for one day, the movie was back on the shelf the next day and rented out again. This not only increased the availability of new movies to satisfy customer demand, it increased our revenue, resulting in more capital available to buy more of the upcoming new releases. And more new releases meant more customer demand. It was an endless loop.

Blockbuster only got credit for a two-day rental from a marketing perspective. Still, the reality was, most of the movies brought back during the evening rush hour didn't make their way to the shelves to be rented out again until the next day. In sum, likely, the new movies rented on a Friday would not be able to be rented again until the following Monday.

To increase the odds of renting our new releases up to three times over the weekend, I installed rolling racks near the check-out counters. We added the labor necessary to immediately check in the returned movies and place them on the racks. I then instructed employees not to waste their time replacing the movies on the walls. There is no better time to re-rent these movies than when the customer was in the store returning the video. And, our return time was not midnight. It was 7:00 PM.

On Saturday nights — the peak rental nights — the top new releases never made it back to the shelves. After dropping off their movies from the day before, customers swarmed the rolling rack in search of new movies recently returned from other customers. It was a turnstile effect, where new releases came in and went right back out in the hands of delighted customers.

When Roger Davidson came on as director of marketing, it allowed us to work directly with an advertising agency and help shape our ads. Knowing the advantage we had over Blockbuster stores, we created the cobweb television ad. The ad focused on our new release availability advantage. Customers were shown pulling movies off our new release wall over and over in fast speed. The wall was being depleted and quickly refilled. It resembled those films of ants bringing back food to the queen in fast motion. We would constantly switch back and forth to a Blockbuster new release wall, depleted and with cobwebs. It was my favorite ad we ever made, but it made me nervous that it would cause Blockbuster to change their ways. To the amazement of everyone on the management team, Blockbuster never did. They stood there like a punching bag, absorbing the blows like Mahamid Ali's rope-a-dope, but never eventually coming out into the middle of the ring to fight, like Ali did.

Our other competitive advantage was how we priced our catalog — the old three-two-one. We rented newer movies waning in rentals for two dollars. Catalog movies, many of which were already paid for many times, were rented for one dollar. This was a substantial discount to the overwhelming majority of movies rented at Blockbuster's stores. Where would you rent? Would it be a store that was dramatically more expensive on eighty percent of their inventory and often out of the new movies you wanted?

Never satisfied, Greg Smith came up with an idea to add fuel to our fire. One day in a strategy session, Greg said, "What if we counter Blockbuster's two-day rentals by letting people rent our hot titles for a week? We have more than we could ever rent out now that they have cooled off, so what does it matter how many days we give them?"

We loved Greg's reasoning but needed to flesh it out more. How many days could we afford to have them out? How would it affect catalog titles? And would the customer find it difficult to have different return dates for other categories? All excellent questions to resolve, and resolve them we did.

We all agreed that hot titles and catalog titles would rent for five days at a time. We didn't want it to be overly complicated, so renting both categories for the same number of days simplified things. Two-thirds of a video store's business falls over Friday, Saturday, and Sunday. We wanted movies rented on the weekend, but back for the following weekend.

Our customers loved it and rented more than ever. It was a real boom for the catalog titles, as the average number of titles being rented exploded. Again we waited for Blockbuster to respond... Crickets.

How many new releases could we *afford* to stock? Another way to say this is, how many new releases can we profitably buy? The average new release costs fifty-four dollars each. New movies were never all rented out on any days other than the first and second weekends and maybe the third Saturday. So the movies at the top of the stack would never bring in more than twenty-one dollars. It was somewhat like driving a new car off the lot and watching its value dump, only new movies had the shelf life of bananas.

Years before, as the dollars spent on new movies exploded — and knowing the importance of getting the initial purchase right — I formed a new movie buying committee. As the rapper Eminem said in his song, "Lose Yourself": *If you had only one shot, one opportunity,* how many new Top Gun movies would you buy? If you overbuy, you are wasting your money. Still, if you under buy, you are not servicing your customer the best you can.

Buying new movies isn't like restocking baked beans. Movies are an art form, with each person having their unique preferences for films. My challenge was to turn art into a science. Math-based but without losing the art form.

This time, with no field of grain in the background, I somehow hatched a plan. I would form a purchasing group with management, which I was sure had diverse taste in movies; I could not leave the purchasing decision to one individual, who would likely use their preference in films to make all of their decisions. I also needed a way to keep their preferences in check, even though they were a part of a group.

I turned to Greg to work with Barry Beitz to utilize the wealth of data stored in the IBM mainframes at corporate. I knew Greg was numbers-based and conversant in computer lingo. His charge was to keep a rental log of every new release we purchased. I did not just want to know how many times we rented them, I wanted to know how many times we rented them over the first eight weeks they were released. My thesis was to target every new movie paying for itself over that eight weeks. Not individually, but rather, as a whole. You can't expect the top movie on the stack in any given store to pay itself off in eight weeks, but you could count on the movies on the bottom of the stack to pick up the slack.

Greg captured the data, and David compiled them into books by categories. We knew there was a relationship between dollars at the box office and rentals in our stores — a relationship between action and drama, even movie actors. They were all unique in their special way. For instance, a movie that did $100,000,000 at the box office did well in our stores because of its popularity. Yet, a significant number of customers had already seen the movie. However, Dolph Lundgren, which did $20,000,000 at the box office and was an action movie, would do more rents per million than a major blockbuster movie. Fewer customers saw it at the theatres, so the film would be new to more people.

The objective was not to put down how many we bought, but the correct amount we should have purchased.

As far as I know, we were the only people in the video rental industry to capture the results in this specific way. Later on, when the movie studios discovered the data we had gathered in our books, they begged us for it. I'm sure they would have paid a pretty penny, but you never want to sell your business secrets.

Once a month, each member of the committee, armed with this information, would sit down at the table for the day. Studios provided us with advance copies, so we divvied them up among the group. Some were horror experts, so they received the horror films, etc. After a full discussion of the different films, each buyer said how many we should purchase. After collecting the votes, we bought the average of everyone's combined order. I've always been a firm believer that the group is smarter than the individual.

To keep everyone honest, Greg kept their predictions on every movie. He graded them eight weeks after the movie's debut in our stores. Not to be mean or embarrass anyone, I had the loser bring lunch at the next buying meeting. I often hoped Art would lose because he made the best Texas chili. We also kept track and gave out plaques for the two top performers at the end of each year. Greg was a regular winner, proving math usually won out.

I felt it was essential to pay close attention to the experts in each genre, using them as a guide if you had not watched the movie. In other words, keep an open mind. My theory was that it would make everyone better at buying. To demonstrate, both Alan Payne and Roger Davidson had to buy lunch three months in a row after joining our committee. To the best of my knowledge, they never did again. Lesson learned.

Our top store was in San Antonio on Wurzbach Road. They typically needed around one hundred copies of $100,000,000 box office hits, as an example. Greg then allocated to the rest of the stores based on their sales volume. Over time, he adapted each store to their customers' buying preferences.

And that is how you buy as many new releases as you can possibly afford.

Our new release walls dwarfed Blockbuster's due to our pinpoint accuracy in buying. It gave us the confidence to step out and live on the edge.

I would like to note that Video Central had a totally different environment than our competition. Walking into a Blockbuster, you found it sterile and quiet. You would hear a movie being played on the monitors in the back of the store. It's almost like you were afraid to talk too loudly. Coming from a music background, I had speakers mounted throughout the stores, playing the latest tunes. In the evenings, the stores were festive. People engaged with one another and our employees, which I believe were a cut above. Extremely well trained and generous, all with a smile. I'm sure this played into our success.

While on competitive advantages, I do not want to dismiss the fact we had the H-E-B logo as part of the name. It was H-E-B Video Central.

We decided to open four stores in Houston, Texas. Fully Clingman explained to me that H-E-B had plans to enter the Houston market at some point, and they did not want the video stores to be the first time customers saw the H-E-B logo. I understood their point of view, but then Fully asked if they could be called Craig's Video Central. I was very leery to accept.

"Are you sure?" I replied.

He was sure, so I acquiesced. After the first store opening, I was in a van with Fully and others I can no longer remember. The van swung by the airport to pick up Charles Butt. While in the van, Charles started ragging me about my name over the door. I didn't know Charles well enough to tell if he was kidding or not. After all, no one had ever had their name over a retail store owned by H-E-B. I wanted to say Fully made me do it, but I stayed silent. To this day, I have no idea if Fully told Charles it was his idea or whether Charles knew and was toying with me.

The Houston stores were profitable but always a notch below stores with H-E-B's name over the door. I say this to demonstrate the impact the H-E-B name had on our success. It was a unique opportunity to have a fully entrepreneurial division operating within a large corporation. The synergy was powerful — a perfect blend of fast-paced entrepreneurial minds with the powerful resources of a top-tier company. We were free to focus on the business, while H-E-B provided the accounting and construction necessary to support our expansion.

And finally, Alan Payne and Robert Najera provided the leadership to develop a store culture second to none. It was a perfect blend of cultures, resulting in the best employees and a real competitive advantage. Five hundred strong!

"*Carpe Diem*. Seize the Day, Boys. Make Your Lives Extraordinary!"
— Dead Poets Society

As a team, we were never satisfied. Blockbuster's primary focus seemed to be on new store openings. We continued to open new stores as well, but we focused on retail first and opening stores second. Everyone on the team came from a retail background — Alan and Roger from H-E-B. Robert, Rick, Dave, Greg, and myself from the entertainment industry. Our primary focus was video rentals, as it was where our major profits came from, but we constantly tinkered around the edges.

Greg had a couple of sayings that summed up how we approached it. "A test is worth a thousand expert opinions," and, "Let the customers vote with their dollars." And that's what we did. All new concepts were tried in our flagship store. And if successful, they were rolled out to the rest of the stores. We all came up with ideas as a group and then relied on Rick from a merchandising standpoint and David to purchase the merchandise.

We tried selling movies, candy, popcorn, records, and even CDs. When the dust settled, it was clear: customers wanted to rent movies and pick up candy and popcorn. They viewed our stores the same way they viewed movie theatres. The only time we ever sold movies was when Disney came out with a new children's title or a major motion picture studio released a major movie priced to sell. Children will watch a single movie over and over. The studios figured a customer would watch a few select motion pictures many times and want to own it in their home video library. We welcomed these movies, not because of the money we could make selling the title, but rather because purchasing a movie for $18 instead of $54 moved the needle on how many we could *profitably purchase for rental*. And that meant greater availability to our rental customers. Another source of revenue from selling movies came from shipping our rental movies we no longer needed to H-E-B supermarkets and promoting them in dump bins at attractive prices.

It was proof that the public would buy movies but not at high prices. But the studios had a conundrum. After fighting to keep retailers from renting videos, they realized they were making too much money. Selling every movie for $18 would cost the studios a fortune and make a tidy sum for the video retail industry. It wasn't until years later, after the adoption of DVDs, that the studios moved to lower prices on *all* movies.

The buying team spent a lot of time watching smaller, lesser-known titles too small and underfunded to make it to the box office. We were watching the movies at home for our own pleasure after one of the committee members tipped us off. Eventually, we realized an opportunity we were overlooking.

The program was called Sleepers. I let each buyer sponsor an overlooked movie. The catch was that they had to write a review. We gave the program prime real estate on the back wall. And we bought ten times the number we would generally have. The independent studios were thrilled, and many of them discounted the movie to us. These smaller titles were already lower-priced than the notable titles, so they became our most profitable movies. And to make it fun for the buyers and customers, I had caricatures made of each buyer and placed at the top of their recommendation. Over time, people learned that they enjoyed particular buying committee members recommendations better than others.

Another program was Warehouse Access. Although our stores carried thousands of movies, there were thousands of movies we could not afford to stock. Greg set up computer terminals at each San Antonio store, and Wanda provided the signage. David filled our warehouse with one of every movie we did not carry in the stores. The customer looked through our warehouse database at a dedicated terminal set up at the store and reserved a movie. Liz's team made van runs twice a week to deliver the product to the stores and pick up overstock and defective videos. The courier dropped off the customer's movie and picked it back up on their next run, somewhat as Netflix did but not through the mail.

The program was marginally successful, and I'm sure the customers that utilized it were appreciative. But so much of renting movies is instant gratification. We let the customers vote with their dollars and eventually discontinued the program. We perhaps pulled the plug too early — the program could have continued to grow, but there was no way of knowing.

I always wanted us to try something new. I encouraged everyone to think outside the box and not worry about the consequences if the idea did not succeed. Art came up with the idea of home delivery. He found a lockbox large enough to hold movies. The customer would call their local store (we only tested in one store), and an employee would deliver the film to the lockbox that the customer hung on their door handle. As with Warehouse Access, the program was marginally successful, and we discontinued it. At the end of the year, we had an awards ceremony to honor the best effort. We spray painted one of Art's lockboxes gold with the inscription, "The

Good Try Award" and presented it to Art as the winner. Art was a good sport, and he talks about it to this day.

"What We've Got Here
is Failure to Communicate!"
— *Cool Hand Luke*

Large corporations are similar to the way large cities are many smaller municipalities grown together. They have different departments, different divisions, and different turf wars. It's just a fact of life that this leads to misunderstandings. It's the nature of the corporate beast.

The reader by now knows the time, effort, and logic behind our new release purchases. But very few outside of our department knew. I once explained it to Charles Butt when I was sitting next to him on a plane ride to Houston. When I finished, Charles thought a moment and said, "My father once told me you never build a church large enough to hold everyone on Easter Sunday." I knew Charles got it!

I walked into an Austin supermarket we had just equipped with video rentals. The program was an immediate success. Store managers loved the video departments because they received thirty percent of the revenue. I walked to the front of the department and noticed the manager walking up a grocery aisle briskly to meet me. I awaited his congratulations and thanks... But his face told a different story.

Apparently not pleased, he pointed his finger at me and said, "Do you realize you ran out of new-releases late Saturday night?" Before the store manager gave me a chance to explain, he added, "We don't run out of bread, and you don't run out of new releases!" He then turned and stomped off back down the grocery aisle. I debated about walking after him, but I thought the better of it. I wanted to tell him those movies cost fifty-four dollars each. If you can't rent them on a Saturday night, when do you think you're going to rent them? We're not in the business of throwing them out like stale bread.

It wasn't long after Ron Denny, the VP of Store Operations, wrote me a letter. Ron is the executive that asked if I would take Alan Payne into video, and I was grateful. But it was a letter telling me I needed to put more new movies in the supermarkets. I had pledged to myself a year back that I would challenge anything that would harm the video operation, knowing grocers didn't understand the complexity of renting videos. For much of their business they decide what to sell and stock the shelves. I knew if I did what they demanded and video suffered, I would get the blame, so I much preferred walking away if forced out. So, I sat down and wrote out a long letter to Ron explaining the movie buying process and why I would not comply. Fortunately, that was the end of that.

H-E-B management had a lot invested in video and were alarmed that sales had slumped. I was summoned to a high-level meeting and told they wanted to place a $1,000,000 ad buy to push sales back up. I knew the ads were not going to move the needle much and the $1,000,000 would hit our expense line. I must have been rubbing Greg's buffalo nickels under the table, because I took another shot at explaining the futility of this move. Midway through my dialogue, the buffalo heard turned back and ran over ME.

We had just come off a summer of great sales. But now we are back into fall school season, and the caliber of titles coming out that fall was not good. Knowing the video studios hold back the best movies for summer and Christmas (what I refer to as, 'shoot while the ducks are flying'). My uncle, Dutch Goulet, taught me that back in 1958, our home was located right on the Laguna Madre in Flour Bluff. Dutch was playing bridge with my dad, granddad, and Dutch's son, Bill. I was playing with my marbles on the floor — which I still have to this day, along with my six shooters (no one can ever claim I have lost all my marbles). Dutch looked out the big picture window that overlooked the bay, jumped up, and ran to the front porch. Naturally, I was curious. So, I followed, getting there in time to see him slam two shotgun shells into his double barrel shotgun that was staged on the front porch railing. He raised his shotgun in the air and took a bead on the poor duck flying over Laguna Shore Road on it's way to a little lake on my dad's property. After retrieving dinner, Dutch calmly went back to playing cards, awaiting his next opportunity.

I followed Fully to his office, not knowing whether the green around his gills was from worrying about video rental sales or me getting run over by the buffalo. Regardless, I asked Fully if I could write on his desk calendar. Turning to July, I circled the week surrounding the Fourth of July and stated that if sales weren't totally back by then, I would quit if he asked. I asked him to trust me, and by the Fourth of July all kids were out of school and the lineup of A-list new releases was back. We had record sales, and all was fine with the world.

I tell this story to illustrate how unique video rentals were. In *Blockbuster: Built to Fail*, Alan Payne describes how Sumner Redstone enticed Bill Fields, the heir apparent and next CEO of Walmart, to quit his job to run Blockbuster. Alan watched Bill revert to what he knew, adding a massive amount of items to sell — not in a test store, as we had, but in the entire chain of Blockbuster stores. Then they got into the electronics business. All a total failure. Who knew?

Later, they hired John Antioco, who turned around Pearl

Vision, Circle K, and Taco Bell. While running Blockbuster, John passed up the opportunity to purchase Netflix because he felt Blockbuster could do it better on its own. Alan knew from talking to John he didn't understand video rental and had no desire to learn from him. If he had listened, he would have learned that franchises who were outperforming corporate Blockbuster stores were doing so because they were operating the Video Central way. Alan was willing to hand the formula over on a silver platter, along with the strides he had made in better understanding the power of carrying a deeper stock of catalogue titles. But John couldn't get his head around a franchise having a better mousetrap than corporate Blockbuster. Alan said in his book that their motto was, "if it didn't come from Blockbuster corporate, it wasn't worth listening to." Talk about arrogance.

I started to believe that if I had a VP title I could better hold my ground. After all, they were already paying me like a VP. I remember the day I saw Alan Markert walking by my office. I yelled after him, "Hey Alan, when is H-E-B going to make me VP?" I said it in a joking manner, but I was not joking. Alan swung around and said, "If you went back to college, got a degree, and then went on to get a masters degree, you could rule the roost at H-E-B!" Walking back into my office I thought, *Well, THAT ain't gonna happen!*

"I'm the King of the World!"
— Titanic

I served on the Video Software Dealers Association (VSDA) National Board in early 1990 – 1993. Supposedly, Wayne Huizenga, Blockbuster's CEO, served as well, but I never saw him at meetings. The only time I did see Wayne was at a video function. I wanted to say hi and maybe chat, so I waited patiently for an opening. Then he came walking across the room in my direction. I was surprised at how short he was. As he approached, I reached out my hand to introduce myself. He paused just long enough for me to tell him I was from H-E-B. Surely, a chance to visit with the company that was crushing them in south Texas would have been of interest. Still, as quick as I had my say, he moved on, disinterested. It made me wonder if he spent any time at all learning about the company he ran.

In 1992, Video Central and The Musicland Group were finalists for the VSDA Video Retailer of the Year Award. It caught H-E-B management's attention that companies like Kmart had been eliminated, yet a small division within H-E-B remained standing. H-E-B allowed us to bring a large Video Central contingency. I was happy that a tier of partners below Video Central management could travel to Las Vegas and be a part of the festivities. They had worked their tails off to build our division, and it would be a nice reward and recognition.

I had become good friends with Gary Ross, a Musicland Group executive, and it provided for friendly competition. During the first board meeting I attended, I went into the parking lot at the break. I had a lot of bets on the football games that weekend and searched for good cell reception. Gary was there, doing the same. It was just one of many common interests we had, developing into a strong friendship we maintain to this day.

On our way into the convention center, I noticed they had big banners with the names of members that attended the first VSDA conventions — a list of the old-timers. I was shocked to find my name on the first convention list in Washington DC with only four other members. That was the moment it dawned on me that I was an early pioneer in the video rental industry. The trip to the VSDA convention was to become the climax of all the hard work everyone in the Video Division had put in over the years. I was pleased they all were having the time of their lives.

Through the years, I had developed a good relationship with our movie supplier, Ingram Video. I can remember the week David Ingram visited us in San Antonio. He was new to the business and learning the ropes before he took control as the President. I also remember meeting David's father in a hotel room around this time. I came away amazed that a man who built a business empire in Nashville, Tennessee, was so humble and approachable. It was no wonder his son was the same way.

In business, I always put a high priority on relationships. Many movie distributors approached us for our business, offering deals a few percentage points lower on VHS tapes. Ingram was already giving us a good price, so it was hard for them to go much lower. I never seriously considered leaving Ingram. Ingram Video, like all video suppliers, went the way of the industry and closed its doors. The last time I talked to David, he had purchased a beer distributorship in California. David laughed and said, "Let them try and digitize alcohol!"

The day before the final event, the President of VSDA notified us that Video Central won the coveted prize of Video Retailer of the Year! I was to give an acceptance speech in front of 5,000 industry participants. Not wanting to embarrass H-E-B, I prepared a speech for the first time in my life. However, I did prepare it while playing a round of golf.

Our management team was seated by the stage, while our rank and file was sitting in the audience. After the honor was announced, I mounted the stage to accept the beautiful silver platter. To my surprise, the lights were shining so brightly on me that I could see very little of the audience. It was like speaking to an empty warehouse. But when I thanked my team and asked them to stand up, the room erupted in applause. We had finally arrived, and H-E-B Video Central was on the map!

The festivities had just begun. Some of us were invited to the penthouse of a hotel. The walls were made of glass, and we could see the lights of Las Vegas sparkling in the distance. The drinks were flowing, and we were hob-knobbing with famous actors. Rick Mulinix and I had an interesting conversation with Edward James Olmos. He had grown up in east LA. Learning we were from San Antonio, Edward told us stories about his visits to Texas and how much he loved San Antonio. Then he whispered, "I can never return because of the Mexican Mafia!"

I caught a glimpse of John Lovitz, who had just starred in the movie *A League of Their Own* with Tom Hanks and Geena Davis. John had played the derelict manager who was ill-prepared to control all the estrogen in the women's team clubhouse. John had a dry, witty, sarcastic humor — much like my own. Okay, maybe mine leans a little more sarcastic than witty, but it's all in a good-humored way.

John was all alone, staring out the window. I walked up and began telling him how much I enjoyed his acting. It took him a while to turn around. He gave no response. I tried something else but realized his eyes were glazed over, as if in a trance. I caught a glimpse of Rick coming our way. Rick had a similar sense of humor, and I could tell he was very excited. I looked at Rick and waved him off, then decided to leave John the way I left the crumpled group of Thin Lizzy band members that morning in Corpus Christi. Once I explained the situation to Rick, he laughed, and we went on our way.

I ran into Gary Ross, and after a bit of good-natured ribbing, Gary was sincerely happy for me winning his award. Gary was well known and liked in the industry, so I'm sure it was a close call. Maybe it was the fact the Musicland stores sold movies in malls and never rented them at the time.

Downstairs, Greg Smith came up to me. "Come on, you're just in time. Lou Diamond Phillips is supposed to address the crowd," he said. We had never met Lou, but we knew he graduated from Flour Bluff High school in 1980, ten years after Greg and me. We were also big fans. We stood in the middle of the crowd, and when Lou came out, we were going to yell, "GO FLOUR BLUFF HORNETS!!!" Then we hoped he would seek us out after his talk. But he never showed.

During the convention, I worked $300 into $2,600. Word got around, and it excited our troop. I've been known to play the black eight on the roulette wheel. And that's where I gave back all but the $300 I arrived with. Word of that got out as well, and I was told the team was crushed. I guess they were living vicariously through me and I felt bad about it. Had I known how much it meant to them, I would have stopped gambling after I was up.

I was exhausted when I got home. Cathie asked me how it went. I told her about our winning Retailer of the Year and my speech. Then I screwed up, saying it might have been the biggest moment in my life. Why are wives so skilled at keeping their husbands grounded? She said with a frown, "You mean bigger than the births of your children?" Now, why didn't I say the biggest moment of my business career? A couple of years earlier, Cathie delivered our last child, Stephen Harper. Our family was complete.

"You Just Gotta Keep Livin,' Man"
— *Dazed and Confused*

When we returned, Charles Butt sent out a letter to the entire company to congratulate our team for our award. Our spirits were at a high, and we were chomping at the bit to open more stores. I had a sit down with Alan Markert and pitched expanding into Arizona. My rationale was that it was understored. Most of the population was in a few markets, and we could get direct flights on Southwest Airlines. The two-hour flight took no more time than traveling to Austin, Houston, or Corpus Christi by car from San Antonio.

It was now 1993, and still no answer — it was a topic H-E-B did not discuss. We plugged along, still the same. Monday meetings were beginning to lose their luster. Something was brewing, but Alan was tight-lipped. Until one day, he wasn't. Video Central was going to be put up for sale to the highest bidder, and we needed to prepare presentations for suitors.

I can't say it was unexpected. The signs had been pretty obvious. Alan Markert said Charles Butt wanted to make sure our management team went with the deal. By now, Roger Davidson had already moved on. Shortly after, Alan Payne was contacted by a Blockbuster franchise, Prime Cable, which was founded by Bob Hughes. They were one of the largest and most successful Blockbuster franchises in El Paso and Alaska. In *Blockbuster: Built to Fail*, Alan states, "As successful as Prime Cable had been, these cable television veterans had no answer when competitors began to steal their Blockbuster customers." Alan goes on to say, "Prime had made many of the same mistakes Blockbuster would repeatedly make in coming years. But unlike Blockbuster, Prime was open to listening to another point of view, especially to someone from H-E-B, a company with which they were familiar."

I remember sitting at the original Rudy's BBQ, eating lunch, when Alan asked me what I thought. We had a good conversation. I told Alan I was happy for him and agreed he should take the opportunity, considering our future at Video Central was uncertain. Alan eventually found an investment group to back his purchase of Primes stores in Alaska and El Paso.

Franchisees could price their movies anyway they saw fit, so Alan began implementing our pricing formula. It wasn't long before Alan's stores were massively outperforming Blockbuster. Alan's stores went on operating for years after the corporate stores shut down. It's a fascinating story and worth reading. If you're interested, you can find *Blockbuster: Built to Fail* on Amazon books.

Around that time, our buyer, David Solar, had been talking to Mark Wattles. Mark was operating a fifteen-store chain out of Portland, Oregon and was peppering David with questions. I learned about it when David walked into my office and said Mark wanted to talk to me. David said that Mark had heard about a thirty-three-store retail chain headquartered in San Antonio that was kicking Blockbuster's butt, and he wanted to find out how. I told David I didn't want to talk to Mark and instructed him not to anymore.

As I was preparing our presentations, I contemplated why we were up for sale. I understood that after selling my company to H-E-B, I was just an employee. H-E-B owned Video Central and could do as they pleased. I did not begrudge them that and would do my best to get them the best price. At that point, I had not yet entertained the idea of finding backing to purchase the stores myself.

Venture capital firms came through one after another. H-E-B had already provided them with financials, so the suitors mainly spent their time asking me operational questions, to which I rattled off the answers.

During the meetings, it became known to me that someone new wanted in on the bidding. Mark Wattles had just taken his company, Hollywood Video, public, and he was working on a secondary, offering to raise more capital. The target was to be the purchase of our Video Central stores. Mark was the only suitor that did not request an interview with me. Maybe because he was in the business himself, or perhaps he thought I would refuse to meet him again. *I'm joking on the last point.*

One of the VCs caught me outside during a break. He wanted to know if I would join them in the bid for Video Central. He explained that he was impressed with my team and me, and we would receive twenty percent of the new company. The idea appealed to me. We would remain in control of the company we built and could expand again. They contacted H-E-B and requested a meeting, which I would have attended. I figured it would be a win-win. Video Central management would be protected, and H-E-B would get their money.

Word got out to Mark Wattles that I was entering the contest for these thirty-three prized stores. Mark called me, and I took his call this time. Mark said he wanted me to fly to Portland. He had a lot of Hollywood Video stock options at his disposal. Mark was trying to buy me off. I refused his invitation because it wasn't in the best interest of my team, and at the time, I felt it was unethical.

"You Talking to Me?"
— *Taxi Driver*

Jack Brouillard, a fairly recent executive hire at H-E-B, asked me to join him for lunch one day. Jack was from the east coast, and to me, he never fit the H-E-B mold. Jack said he would pick me up in the corporate parking lot, which felt a little strange. As strange as this east coaster pulling up in a pickup truck. Maybe that was his attempt to fit in.

At lunch, Jack acknowledged my attempt to join forces with the VC firm, but he pretty much glossed over it. Then he started to tell me that Mark Wattles and I would set the video industry on fire. A dynamic duo! His message was clear, so I didn't press the issue. If I did press the issue, it wouldn't be with him. But I began to wonder if Jack was the man behind the curtain pulling strings.

After lunch, Jack pulled up in front of my car. I was looking forward to getting out, but he stopped me for one last word. With a stern voice, he said, "If anyone tries to kill the deal we have with Hollywood, *I will personally cut their nuts off.*"

Yep, he was talking to me.

I sat in my car, attempting to process what just transpired. I thought about all I had given to the Video Division. I entered the race late, but at least why not let the process play out? But the entire process took place without my participation. Even though I was in the dark every step of the way, I gave my all to ensure H-E-B got a fair offer.

When it all sunk in, I felt disrespected. It was time to take matters into my own hands, and Jack had just laid down the ground rules.

I drove back to our offices and told Greg Smith, my long-time friend and business partner, to pack his bags. We were going to Portland. I went into the bathroom and noticed I had cut myself shaving that morning and had dried blood on my neck and white shirt collar. Or was that from Jack?

"I'm Going to Make You an Offer You Can't Refuse"
— *The Godfather*

Mark Wattles and Scott South picked us up at the airport and drove us on a tour of their fifteen stores. As the CFO, Scott was the nuts and bolts behind all day-to-day operations. He was a very competent man.

Mark had an excellent store designer. The Hollywood Video stores were visually superior to Video Centrals, but Greg and I never let on. We noticed Mark had copied our three-two-one pricing formula, and the walls were heavily stocked with new releases.

Mark had a flair about him. He could have given P.T. Barnum a run for his money as a promoter. Flamboyant might be the word best to describe him. Mark impatiently turned back to me from the passenger seat and wanted to get down to business. But he made a colossal mistake. Mark started the negotiations by telling me ALL the options Hollywood Video had. Some would immediately vest at a penny a share. A more significant portion vested over three years and was marked to the stock price when you received it. He then asked, "How many will it take for you to drop out of the bidding process?"

The entire time in the car, I never once brought up a word about my involvement in the bidding process for Video Central, and I never did throughout our visit. I immediately replied, "All of them!"

Mark's mood changed. He had a threatening tone. I honestly

can't remember all he said. Greg and I sat in the back seat quietly. Once Mark cooled down, he said to Scott's chagrin, "Okay, I'll give you all of them." That told us Mark wanted Video Central bad. And there was a good reason, which I will explain later.

Two of our VC buddies had flown out to Portland the following day. They realized they had lost and wanted to build a business relationship with Hollywood Video. Mark met us at a restaurant the next night to close the deal. Greg and I were fortunate enough to have them along because they penned out an official contract to bring with them.

We made small talk until Mark asked, "Are we going to do this or not?" We handed Mark the contract, and he quickly looked it over. Fortunately, for our whole management team and us, the VC asked Mark for one dollar to make the contract binding.

I say whole management team because Mark thought we were taking the options all for ourselves. He was surprised when we took half and divided up the rest with our long-time associates. Many had been with me since the record days, and some were hired from H-E-B. The options ensured my compatriot's safe passage to Hollywood Video and rewarded them for their hard work. I imagine Mark might have given them some stock options on his own, but that's not guaranteed, and nothing in the range of what they received.

I felt good about how things transpired and that it didn't cost H-E-B one red cent. Everything came from Hollywood Video's coffers.

"I Want to Be Alone"
— *Grand Hotel*

The Video Central transaction closed with Hollywood Video. Mark and his team were coming to town. The word from Alan Markert was that Mark would try and get some of his stock options back. Mark wanted to meet for breakfast, so I took him to one of my favorite Mexican restaurants.

As Mark talked, I enjoyed my huevos rancheros and tallied my arsenal. First, the contract was well written and legally binding. Second, Mark was trying to complete another secondary offering. I knew it would be hard for him to close with a lawsuit pending, but Mark was unaware that I knew. I was willing to call his bluff if need be.

By then, I decided not to go to Portland with Hollywood Video. The bulk of my stock options were the penny options that would vest immediately. It was my stock options he was after, so I knew my crew was safe. Because I was not going to Portland, the stock options that required me to work for Hollywood Video and vest overtime were of no value to me.

I finished my breakfast. I looked across the table and told Mark that I had come up with what I thought was fair. There would only be this one offer, and if he disagreed, I was prepared to take him to court. I said, "I will keep the penny stock options and give you back the others." Mark agreed with no further discussion.

I could never have imagined the effect breaking up with my team would have on me. I'm not an emotional person by nature, but I felt like I had lost a loved one. I couldn't bring myself to go into the office the last two days. I needed to sort it out, and it would take time. Wanda organized a final getaway with the team in Bandera, Texas. I had regained my composure enough to attend, but I somewhat sleepwalked through it. I still have the beautiful branding iron with the Video Central logo mounted on a rustic piece of wood that the crew gave me. It hangs over my easy chair as I type this book.

Video Central had a phantom stock option plan that vested upon closing the deal with Hollywood Video. I had forgotten all about it. After everyone in management received their checks, I asked where mine was. When I was told I would not be receiving my share, I was astonished. So I went straight to the top, sending Charles Butt an email inquiring as to why. Charles said that no one that ever worked for H-E-B left with as much money as I had. He was referring to the stock options.

Never knowing how much Charles knew about what had transpired, I replied with a full rundown. Especially the part about Jack Brouillard telling me he would cut my nuts off. Several days later, Charles sent a reply saying he agreed that I was entitled to the $200,000.

My relationship with Charles and H-E-B meant a lot to me. I didn't want to end it on a sour note, so I responded to Charles with a letter saying his response meant a lot to me and that I would pass on my phantom stock allocation. I came out in good financial condition and figured God had a plan in store for me. As it turned out, this would not be the last business relationship I had with H-E-B.

The purchase of Video Central was well received on Wall Street. On the announcement, Hollywood Video's stock jumped from seven dollars a share to twenty-one dollars a share. Hollywood was now a regional chain, and the massive cash flow from the Video Central stores would fund many new Hollywood Video stores to come.

"Just When I Thought I Was Out... They Pull Me Back In"
— The Godfather: Part III

Six months later, I received a phone call from Mark Wattles. Mark wanted to fly me to Portland and pick my brain. We mostly drove around in his car as he asked my opinions. At one point, we stopped, and I met his father. After I returned to San Antonio, Mark called again. He said that when he talked to me, I made a lot of sense, and he offered me a job: Executive Vice President of Hollywood Video.

Cathie is very close to her three sisters, Linn, Tricia, and Nancy. And even closer with her parents, Bet and Jack. And they were all located in San Antonio, Corpus Christi, Houston, and Austin. I hesitated to relocate my family, but even Cathie thought it was too good of an opportunity to pass up.

I left immediately and would have them join me when school had a semester break. Hollywood Video had leased the original Nike headquarters, and Mark's office used to be Phil Knight's. Mark never told me exactly what my job responsibilities were, so I started with what I knew best: new release purchasing.

Mark had a used movie broker named Joe Jennigas running purchasing. He was a good guy, but when I asked him how much they reinvested in new releases, I got a blank stare. So, I went to visit Scott South, the CFO. I got the same blank stare. Scott said he would crunch some numbers and get back to me.

As you know, we were very sophisticated with our new release purchases at Video Central. We never set a percentage number we were trying to hit because we knew we were more efficient

140

in purchasing videos than anyone. The number always seemed to average out to thirty-five percent of revenue. After taking out rent, wages, marketing, etc. eighteen percent went to the bottom line. Several days later, Scott reported they had been re-investing seventy percent to new releases. The number floored me! Houston, we've got a problem. They were most likely running a negative seventeen percent cash flow.

Movies were capital expenditures, and as such, were depreciable assets. H-E-B found a way to write them off immediately. Still, a public company like Hollywood Video would want to depreciate them over time. Most likely over three years. Three years enables them to delay the hit to earnings and look more profitable. But even at three years, spending seventy percent would catch up to them in a hurry. I knew there was a head-on collision with a freight train coming down the tracks. My best estimate was that they had about six more months before it slammed their earnings.

I walked immediately to Joe and asked him to explain to me how he purchased new releases. He said that he held a monthly new release meeting. His representative from the distributor he purchased his movies from would bring a list of movies for that month and the recommended amount. Joe said he would "massage the numbers a bit" (whatever that meant) and place the order. In my view, it was like letting the fox into the hen house. The rep had everything to gain by recommending more movies to buy.

I explained to Joe that he should respectfully dis-invite the rep to our purchasing meetings. I then went into the back offices to look up Rick Mulinix and Art Seago, the two Video Central veterans that had moved to Portland. Without Greg Smith and the IBM mainframes, we devised a method to replicate our old program on Microsoft Excel the best we could. They both had been a part of the Video Central buying committee. The three of us had a good handle on how many of each movie to buy based on our past experiences. Not wanting to bring a shock to the system, we decided to shoot for fifty percent and then gradually get the reinvestment rate back down to thirty-five percent a little at a time.

With Art and Rick handling the new buying system, I looked around for more to do. Mark still had everyone other than Joe reporting to him. Mark never held weekly meetings, as I did at Video Central. They were one-on-one sessions with his lieutenants. I was not present, so I was pretty much out of the loop. He never gave me any directions or explained what he wanted from me. Nor did he ask my opinions. I was not privy to financial decisions. If he and Scott were having a meeting and I walked in, Mark stopped talking. I knew a ticking time bomb was coming. Massively over-purchasing newly released movies during the six months between the Video Central buyout and my arrival would have grave repercussions.

Mark spent most of his time talking to analysts, and he was good at it. I suppose that is how things are in a publicly-traded company, but it made me feel uneasy. My style would have been to run the business from the ground up, making the best business decisions I could, and then let the stock price reflect how well the decisions were made. I worried Mark was too focused on the stock price of Hollywood Video, but that was not my call.

An executive meeting further drove home this point. Mark wanted to purchase a fifty-store chain in Wisconsin. I listened to his pitch and tried to make sense out of it. My analysis was that the chain was operating in an area Blockbuster had not yet built out. The stores were lower volume due to their inferior store locations. I feared Blockbuster would come in with bigger stores and better locations, putting a squeeze on the stores. And Mark was paying almost as much as he paid for our video stores.

I didn't say much until Mark told us he had agreed to pay the same amount for twelve locations that only had a signed lease. We still had to pay for the buildout and the movies. They had no operating revenue. I could hold my tongue no more.

I lobbied for either not purchasing the chain or driving a harder bargain. I added that in no uncertain terms should we pay for stores that were not yet open. Mark listened and then did it anyway. His reasoning was that the purchase was valid because it would boost the stock price of Hollywood Video. My suspicions were confirmed. His decisions were being made primarily on the price of the stock. In my opinion, Mark was making the same mistake Blockbuster was making.

I knew from experience that Blockbuster was more interested in how many stores they built, spending little time on the competitiveness of their stores. Hollywood Video had one advantage: they were highly competitive because of our Video Central pricing model.

By now, I had moved Cathie and the kids into a beautiful home on five acres. The kids were back in school, but looking back, not locating them in a subdivision was a mistake. Cathie was isolated, and the kids missed their friends. Cathie missed her family even more. Portland, Oregon, is a beautiful place because of how green it is. But it is green because of constant rain. Days were getting shorter, the skies were always cloudy, and the chill was intense. At night, I had to draw a tub of hot water to get the cold out of my bones before bed. Unless you grew up there, it was unbearable.

My days at Hollywood Video became monotonous, and I came home to an unhappy family. It was time to decide between family and business. It was an easy choice. We put the house on the market before I even told Mark. A couple who wanted the place when we purchased it found out the property was back on the market. It sold in one day. Was it a sign?

Visiting with the realtor, we learned that there was a pattern of Texans moving to Oregon only to pick up and move back shortly after. Before we left, Mark was invited on a fishing trip to Mexico by David Ingram. Mark did not want to go, so he asked me to go in his place. Mark was not into fishing, and he knew David would like to push for his business. I became uncomfortable with the situation in Nashville and leveled with David. Cathie and I were leaving Hollywood Video and headed back to San Antonio. Confiding in David somewhat soured the trip, and when David called Mark, he was not pleased. But hey, I was on my way out anyway.

After I sent Cathie and the kids back to San Antonio, I was preparing to leave myself. Mark asked me to take a drive with him. He said he needed me to stay for two more years. His comment about a specific time made me think my being there was all a show. I had an excellent relationship with the movie studios — maybe it had a positive impact on business analysts. I guess I will never know because I said no.

I was mentally exhausted and couldn't wait to mount my dark green Landcruiser to drive home. I needed time to myself, so I took a route over the mountain range, through the deserts of Oregon, and down remote Nevada territory. As I hit the flatlands, I put on "Born to Run' by Bruce Springsteen, and it invigorated me. It was so desolate that I seldom passed a car. When I had to go, I would stop my cruiser on the road and pee on the yellow stripes. My surroundings were flat tabled mountains, just like in John Wayne movies. I was in the badlands, and couldn't have been happier.

Northern Nevada was a valley lined with mountains on either side. It may have been a godforsaken country, but it was beautiful to me. At dusk, I looked in my rearview mirror to see flashing lights approaching at a fast pace. So fast, I decided to pull over. Two black Suburbans with heavily tinted windows led a flatbed truck with a long, concealed projectile, followed by two more black Suburbans. I surmised they were moving a nuclear warhead to a new location.

When we left San Antonio, we loved our home so much that we decided to rent it out. Cathie had spent time designing and meeting with the builder. She had a lot invested. A friend of ours, Roy Terracina, lived a few houses up and was a good friend of Doc Rivers, so he asked us to rent to Doc. It was fortunate because the San Antonio Spurs were in the playoffs, and as soon as they were over, we could move back in. It's probably the only time I rooted for the Spurs to lose. Robert and Tricia were kind, and they let us crash at their home, but it was stressful for all.

Scott South, the CFO of Blockbuster, left weeks after I left Hollywood Video. One quarter later, Hollywood Video released earnings. They announced a one-time extraordinary write-down. The maneuver is a trick public company's use to write off losses as if the losses were extraordinary events beyond their control. I knew Mark was unloading the millions of dollars of depreciation from the over-purchasing of new releases. It worked. The price of his stock went up. Wall Street knows that when a company takes these write-downs, it's a good sign. Past sins get swept under the rug, and they can meet their profit targets in the coming quarters.

"The Song Remains the Same"
– Led Zeppelin

I became good friends with Morris Miller, the founder of Rackspace, a highly-successful cloud storage company in San Antonio. Morris was good friends with Doug Harrison, the entrepreneur that built The Scooter Store. Doug's mobility wheelchairs were of great benefit to those in need, and he found a way for the government to pay for them. All he had to do was dig for the statute. He didn't write it, he just found it. You have undoubtedly seen their advertisements on late-night television.

I had been helping Doug open retail stores in Walmart for about fourteen months when I received a call from Morris Miller. Morris was playing the matchmaker again. He asked me to call Paul Posner. Paul had successfully built Discount Cellular and Paging when cellphones were in their infancy. You remember, the ones the size of a brick? He sold his stores to AT&T, freeing him to look for another project. The US government had an auction to sell cellular spectrums. Paul scooped up spectrums in San Antonio and south Texas on the cheap one auction. And now he was going to build out his own cellular company. Cricket Communications was eying south Texas, so Paul wanted to open first. At the time, Cricket and MetroPCS were building out the entire country. They wisely stayed out of each other's markets to keep competition low. As a result, Cricket was operating like Blockbuster and focusing mostly on growth and little on competitiveness. Knowing they would be the only one in markets, Cricket typically opened with very few stores. Paul's strategy was to open with dozens of stores, guns blazing.

And part of that strategy would be opening kiosks in H-E-B supermarkets the way I did with video rentals in 1982. Only H-E-B didn't know Paul and were not cooperating.

I agreed to attend Paul's last meeting with H-E-B to stem the tide. It felt good being back in their corporate offices. Many memories flashed through my head as I entered the meeting room run by an old friend, Jodi Kerksie. Jodi confided in me later that I was the only reason they agreed to a contract. Paul offered me a job as VP of Store Operations, and I took it. Once again, I found myself working with H-E-B!

My title was VP of Store Operations, but in reality, I wore many hats. My scope was designing and building out fifteen store locations, designing a two-foot by six-foot kiosk for the H-E-B stores that could display the phones, store the inventory, and transact the sale. I was also purchasing all handsets, hiring and training 200 salespeople. There were to be fifteen retail stores and forty H-E-B kiosks.

Fortunately, I hired a strong right-hand man — Eddard Stark, strong. Neil Campbell complimented me perfectly with different skill sets. He was a wizard with Excel and remained behind in the office, freeing me to roam San Antonio. After a few months, I found out Neil was a son-in-law to Bob Loeffler (the ex-President of H-E-B). Now it made perfect sense. Wayne Jahn joined us, assisting in setting up the stores. He was a young man with a great work ethic.

About three months in, Cathie and I took a weekend trip to Miami. We were having a wonderful time when Paul called me. I had no idea, but Cricket was negotiating with Paul behind the scenes, claiming they wanted to buy him out or merge operations in south Texas. I had wondered why things had slowed down a bit, but now it made sense.

Paul is an extremely competitive guy. Not someone you want to cross. He had just found out Cricket was stalling for time so they could try and open ahead of Paul. By now, Paul's company name was Pocket Communications. He told me he had sent them a package. No, it wasn't a horse's head or a little pinky, but I can assure you Cricket executives got the message. It was game on!

The next nine months were a blur. Paul managed the technical side, and I took care of the retail side. Towards the end, I brought in an old acquaintance from The Scooter Store, Rudy Martinez, to get the call center up and running. I can remember the excitement of waiting an extra day for "all systems go" before launching. It felt like we were NASA anticipating a rocket launch.

As with the race with Blockbuster to open our new Video Store, we beat Cricket open by a month. Pocket Communications signed up cellular customers by the tens of thousands before Cricket even opened their first store. I stayed on to open a large store in Laredo, Texas but then felt it was time to move on. I did not look forward to the day-to-day operations of an industry I knew little about, and I had already done the heavy lifting. It was time to move on.

"It's the Final Countdown!"
— Europe

Morris Miller sold his shares in Rackspace and started an investment company named Sequel Ventures. He invited me to join him. My job was to come up with a retail venture that I could run. I spent time traveling the country searching for a new idea and meeting with young entrepreneurs Morris had brought in. I found a few business ideas, like a heavy equipment leasing franchise in El Paso, Texas, but nothing stuck. Then H-E-B came calling again.

Pocket Communications was expanding to the Rio Grande Valley. Like video rentals, they decided they wanted to be a cellular retailer for all brands of phones. Pocket would be one of them. They inquired about contracting me to build out the kiosks in their valley stores. I told them I could, but they would be hiring me through Sequel Ventures and they had to fly me home on weekends. The three-month project not only covered my salary but everything Sequel had paid me to date. Then it was back to the office to continue the search.

Morris asked me to investigate a local franchise that was in its early stages of start-up. Massage Heights was, well, a retail massage operation. The massage industry was following the way other retail businesses had done. Replace a mom-and-pop company with nationally-run chains. The new stores were big, clean, and friendly. And they operated on a monthly membership like health clubs.

I visited with Massage Heights management, who sent me to visit their Houston franchise. The franchise was very open and helpful. They had five stores up and running and many more on the way. I liked the fact that it was on the ground floor and how the business compared to video rental. I viewed the business as renting out rooms (real estate) by the hour. The masseuses got paid a nominal base salary for every hour they worked, and the client doubled that with a tip. The monthly rates brought in a guaranteed revenue stream even if the customer did not frequent the location that month.

Morris asked to work out a special franchise fee for the entire state of Arizona. I came back with a franchise fee of three percent of the revenue instead of the asking price of six percent. I felt it was the opportunity we had been waiting to develop. Still, Morris couldn't overcome the stigma of running a massage business, so we passed.

Part of my job was to monitor the business newsletters around the country online. It was early 2008, I believe, and the headlines were all the same. The housing markets were crashing. I reported to Morris, and we knew trouble was brewing but didn't know how to capitalize. Looking back, it may have been a bad idea to launch a retail chain when the economy was getting ready to crash. It was not the time to open any new venture, so I stepped down.

I want to take the opportunity to thank Dan Elder, who I met at Sequel Ventures, and who eventually took my place. Dan is one of the warmest men you will ever meet, and I'm grateful to him for unselfishly helping my son, Stephen, with his new business venture.

And then there came a fitting ending to my time working with and for H-E-B!

In 2009, my wife Cathie was nominated for the Excellence in Education Award in the "Rising Star" category and won. H-E-B sponsored the event and Charles was a big supporter of educators and education.

I proudly traveled with her to Austin, Texas. I stood against the back wall of the room as she lined up to accept her award. Charles Butt walked in and congratulated each teacher warmly as they reached him. When it was Cathie's turn, they embraced each other. Charles wished her well, and said, "Tell the big guy hi for me."

This is a picture of my family's Dairy Queen, taken when I was very young. This is where all of the Flour Bluff High kids hung out!

My parents, Steve and Jane, standing outside of what was left of their Dairy Queen after Hurricane Celia hit.

*My high school basketball team. Front row (left to right): Joe Linscomb,
Woodie Jelks, Bill Fette, Orlando Martinez, and Charles Gray. Second row
(left to right): Eric Marhol – Manager, Earl Monroe, Jimmy Kaylor, John
Sebastian, Ronald Malone, myself, David Schuford, and Coach Beard.*

*The Original Craig's House of Music across from the Padre Staples Mall.
This is where it all started!*

Myself, Sandi Carl, and Jim Elliot behind the check out counter at Craig's House of Music.

The Craig's House of Music Team.
(Left to right) Mary, Bob, myself, Al, George, Pat, Jim, and Susan.

BACKSTAGE

CHRISTOPHER CROSS
CONCERT

CRAIG'S
RECORD FACTORY

Sunday, March 16, 1980

PASS

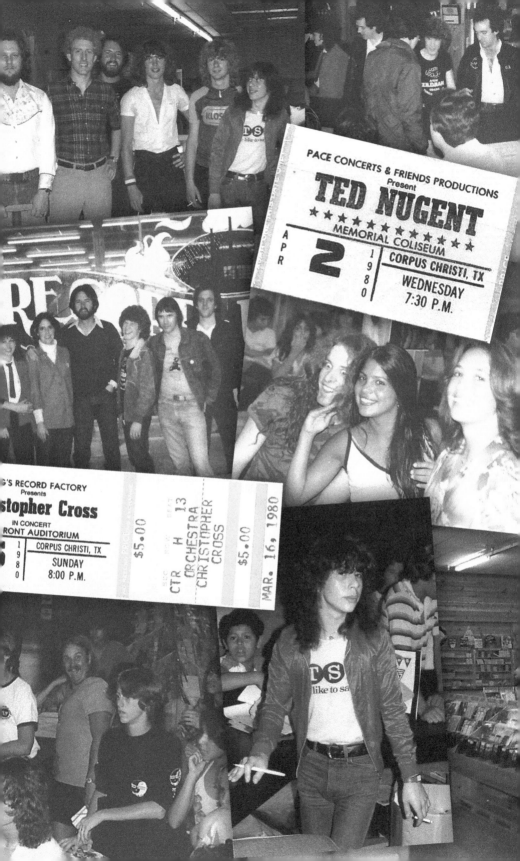

PACE CONCERTS & FRIENDS PRODUCTIONS
Present

TED NUGENT
★ ★ ★ ★ ★ ★ ★ ★ ★

MEMORIAL COLISEUM

APR
2
1980

CORPUS CHRISTI, TX

WEDNESDAY
7:30 P.M.

G'S RECORD FACTORY
Presents

stopher Cross
IN CONCERT
RONT AUDITORIUM

CORPUS CHRISTI, TX

SUNDAY
8:00 P.M.

$5.00

$5.00

CTR H 13
ORCHESTRA
CHRISTOPHER CROSS

MAR. 16, 1980

The Craig's Record Factory logo was displayed proudly on the back mirror of the store.

Roy Smith, my friend who created the Craig's Record Factory logo, modeling a CRF t-shirt.

The Odanovision Inc. Team. (Left to right) Robert Najera, Diane Klovstad, Orlando Martinez, Jane Odanovich, Steve Odanovich, Liz James, myself, Dave Solar, Jaun Martinez, and Patti Simpson.

(Right) A group picture from our Video Central ten year reunion.
(Left) Our mascot, H-E-Bear.

(Left) The March 1991 edition of Video Store Magazine. H-E-B's Video Central was featured, and the edition was titled "Video Central Rides Hard."

(Bottom) This photo was taken in Las Vegas when Video Central won the VSDA Retailer of the Year Award. I am pictured with a Holllywood actor (left) and Eric Doctorow (right), the Executive Vice President of Paramount Home Video.

★ H-E-B ★
VIDEO CENTRAL
CAPTURES
★ VSDA ★
"Retailer of the Year"
★ HONORS ★

by
Orlando Martinez

At the 1992 VSDA Convention in Las Vegas held during July, H-E-B Video Central was among five winners awarded the "Retailer of the Year" title at the "Homer" Awards Banquet.

H-E-B Video Central was selected as the top retailer in the non-specialty category by the VSDA's Manufacturer Advisory Committee. The committee is made up of the following companies: Buena Vista Home Video, Fox Video, LIVE Home Video, MCA/Universal Home Video, Orion Home, Paramount, RCA/Columbia Pictures, and Warner Home Video. The committee based their decision on the following criteria:

* New Product Awareness
* Inventory Commitment Breath/Depth
* Sell-thru Commitment
* Cooperation on Vendor Merchandising Programs
* Vendor Communication
* Fiscal/Ethical Responsibility
* Advertised Product Stocking and Visibility
* Training/Quality of Personnel
* Advertising and In-store Display Tie-in

The VSDA is a non-profit international trade association that is comprised of 4,500 retail, manufacturers, distributors, and other related businesses that make up the home video industry.

Craig Odanovich (left), Video's general manager, posed with actor/director Edward James Olmos (American Me).

VIVA LAS VEGAS! Video Central Managers attended this year's VSDA Convention in 'Vegas. Pictured above (L. to R.): Jerry Briones, Gracie Quintanilla, Pat Davila, Orlando Martinez, Irene Cortez, Leo Trevino, and Jon Jennings (not pictured).

H-E-B Video Central's announcement
that we won the VSDA Retailer of the Year Award.

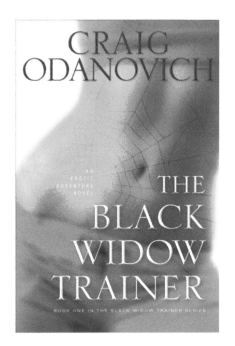

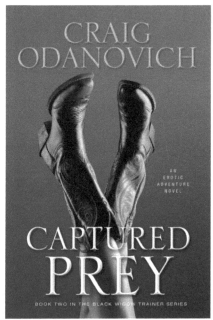

(Top) The cover of my first book, The Black Widow Trainer. (Bottom, left to right) The covers for my second book, Captured Prey, and my third book, Hanging by a Thread.

I am now going to switch gears to discuss a different aspect of my career. Up until this point, I have focused on my journey as an entrepreneur and working within the music and video industry. In many ways, this new project was built off the same character traits that led me to open my first business; passion, and the willingness to take risks. Only this time, I was venturing into a whole new territory. I began writing a book, and not just any book but a series of erotic thrillers I called The Black Widow Trainer *series. The remainder of this book is going to involve excerpts from the series along with my journey writing the novels.*

The Black Widow Trainer Cliff Notes

Late in 2008, the stock market began to give up the ghost along with the housing market. Companies were cutting workers, and the capital markets were freezing up. By now, I was accustomed to laying low and biding my time until another opportunity came knocking, so I decided to spend more time in the gym. I was an avid weightlifter in my younger years, and now at fifty-seven years of age, I felt this might be my last go at reclaiming my former physique. The long workdays, working my tail off at Pocket Communications, had taken their toll. At thirty pounds overweight, it would take dedication and effort. After watching other members make progress with a trainer, I gave way and got one too.

After three months, the muscle mass was back, but I was still not satisfied; I added a daily testosterone diet. Not exactly a diet, rather a gel I applied to my upper body. The workouts became more intense with the new burst of energy, and the results were gratifying. By the end of the year, I was as strong as I had ever been. It's not like I am the only man that has experienced a mid-life change. I don't want to refer to it as a mid-life crisis. There was no crisis. It was simply the realization that my time as a younger, more muscular man was coming to a close. It was self-imposed and personal. Just like no one can tell you how great it is to have grandchildren until you experience holding your grandchild in your arms, no one can explain to a man what happens in mid-life until you reach mid-life.

I observed the same trainers and their clients: the friendships, the shared goals, and the sharing of personal information while spending so much time in the gym. One day I saw a storyline. It was as simple as a young female trainer that had fallen in with rich and powerful men who paid handsomely for her services. Her reputation had spread, and before long, she traveled the world. Each chapter would take place with new clients, new locations, and new characters. I thought in terms of a movie but did not know how to write a screenplay. I didn't know anything about writing. I was a poor speller — still am — and paid little attention in English class. *But I learned how to type! Thank you, Mr. Massingale.*

I've talked to friends that held off writing a book because they were inexperienced and didn't know how to begin. But if you don't begin the process, you will never know if it's for you. So, that's what I did. One day I sat down and laid down a few chapters, and then it was off to the races. I didn't initially approach it as needing to create a complete storyline. I just wanted to get the story going and see where it led. Well, it led to Misty, a married woman having an affair on a trip to Hawaii. She had not planned to have an affair with the mysterious and gorgeous man from Maui. It was seduction.

Guilt swept while riding home from the airport with her husband, Rob. Rob was a great guy, but older and in over his head with Misty. He had known it for a while. Now Misty was waking up to the fact. Later, during a walk on the beach, she had an open heart-to-heart with Rob. He had been dreading this event for several years and knew it was coming, but now it was upon him. Desperate to hang onto Misty, he proposed an arrangement that allowed her to see other men while still living with him. He was desperate to stay in her life.

Throughout the books, I often relied on real people I knew as the basis for my characters. I took their mannerisms and blew them up into larger-than-life characters. In this instance, I used my friend, Rick Mulinix, who was with me from the record days through the Hollywood Video days. Rick is a very even keel, a nice guy, and nice looking. He was not flamboyant. Just a great and dependable guy.

Misty was training Eddie, a handsome and wealthy middle-aged man. One day she confided in Eddie about her affair. But Eddie had been waiting for his opportunity and seized upon it. He invited her to come with him on his trip to Zurich over the next three months to continue to train him. She laughed in disbelief, but he was dead serious. To entice Misty to come with him, he encouraged her to come up with a fee and list of demands.

Misty and Rob had financial problems and could use the money. Rob knew he had given her the freedom, and the opportunity to get out of debt was alluring. While Rob was gone that night, she sat down at the table to get Eddie off her back. She would make a list of demands he would most assuredly turn down. Five thousand dollars for a two-hour session, a fancy rental car, and a stay in a high-end hotel. That would teach him.

Here is an excerpt from *The Black Widow Trainer* describing how this played out at the beginning of their next training session:

When Eddie showed up, Misty ushered him into her office.

"Okay, Eddie, just remember, you said not to be bashful."

He took the document and turned straight to the signature page. Eddie handed Misty the pen and said, "Sign it!"

"But you haven't even read it!"

Eddie took back the pen and signed over his name, handing it back to Misty. "Sign it."

Misty's hand trembled as she signed her name, handing it back to Eddie. Eddie said, with a business tone, "Pack your bags; we leave tomorrow," and turned to walk away.

Rob was in disbelief. He did not want Misty to go, but was enamored with the amount of money she would make. Knowing it was her decision, he made just one demand. Hire Miguel, a young trainer at the club who had grown up in a rough Los Angeles neighborhood, to go as her bodyguard. So, she did.

Misty knew for that kind of money Eddie wanted to sleep with her. She told him that she would let him sleep with her, but only once. The moment he did, she would get paid in full and could go home. If he wanted her full services as a trainer, he would have to wait until the end of three months. Like a black widow spider mating, it was one and done, only he wouldn't die like the male spider. And her goal was to make it hard for Eddie to resist her. Both as a way to go home early and, to some degree, stay in control.

And so the story was born. Eddie couldn't wait, but his real goal was to share her with his rich client friends. He felt once she got the taste of the money, he would have her trapped in his web. It wasn't until years after I finished writing the trilogy that I realized the storyline was somewhat similar to the 1993 film, *Indecent Proposal*, with Robert Redford, Demi Moore, and Woody Harrelson.

I decided to write the chapters about real places. At first, I used places I had already been to, like Beaver Creek, Colorado, and New Orleans. I thought it would provide the reader with somewhat of a defacto travel guide. Unfortunately, my publisher said I could not use establishments' real names. In the end, I spent one whole day making up new names. But I felt between the description of the places and coming up with names not too dissimilar, people could have fun figuring it out.

I wanted to make each adventure different, getting inspiration from the locations and experiences; skiing in Beaver Creek, the feel of the French Quarter and bars in New Orleans, etc. The only time I deviated was the Argentina adventure. I used the internet and Wikipedia to research the area, traditions, and local places. The Argentina chapter came out well, to my astonishment. I think it was the chapter where I hit my stride as a writer. But that did not deter me from going back to my original plan of being on the ground.

To change things up, I had Misty trained by a sophisticated land developer who lived in a mansion overlooking where the Atlantic Ocean meets the Rio de la Plata that runs to Buenos Aires. You can imagine Misty's surprise when her client, M. G. Marquez, turned out to be a toned and attractive woman. The G turned out to be for Gabriella, to Misty's surprise and dismay. Gabriella was assertive but in a fine-spoken, sophisticated way. She bought Misty clothes without asking, insisted Misty learn to tango, and controlled her schedule after work, and at play.

Here is an excerpt from *The Black Widow Trainer* with a physical description of Gabriella as Misty sees her at the first workout:

Misty spotted Gabriella walking through the garden towards the exercise room, skin glowing under light perspiration. Gabby, as Misty later referred to her, was stunning. Her small but muscular frame walked tall at five foot eight and was powered by long, lean leg muscles. She had inherited her Italian mother's olive skin, which beautifully complemented her jet-black hair. Her eyebrows arched over dark brown eyes, making her look alert and intelligent.

She lifted her face to the veranda and waved to Misty, smiling warmly. Gabriella's full lips and button nose made a striking combination. Misty's gaze followed Gabriella's long neck to her sports bra, which hugged her small, firm breasts. Her bare abdomen suggested she was a woman accustomed to working out, as did her lean legs and firm bottom.

Before moving on to other travels, I'd like to mention that Misty is a flawed protagonist, and I never meant her to be the story's hero. She's been unfaithful, but never was a person to be married or tied down. Misty is not a superhero. She doesn't know how to fight or shoot and can be vulnerable when danger approaches. However, Misty does not have a mean bone in her body. She is fast-paced and seizes every moment of the day with little concern for tomorrow.

Misty's friends adore her and are willing to do whatever it takes to protect her. She makes them feel alive when they are near her. And her list of friends grows from chapter to chapter. Many characters end up in subsequent books. Misty's character arc grows over the entire 900-page trilogy, and she learns from her experiences and the people who care about her. I think the reader will be pleased with her growth through her journey. In fact, at the end of the third book, I felt her development complete. Amends made and on her own, she figured out where she truly belonged. I knew I was through writing at that moment. To move forward would have only been retrograde steps. And who wants to read about Misty's perfectly happy, normal life? Where's the fun and intrigue in that?

Riding from San Antonio to El Paso and back with my good friend, John Kuderer, we discussed my upcoming trip to Alaska. John was friends with my cousin, Kevin West, who in real life is the brother I never had, and his best friend, Mike Peterson. Kevin and Mike have been best friends for life, and each one had his own unique character. Jokingly, we cast them for Alaska, which was to be a wild and crazy place. Something Misty had never experienced before, and for most of the adventure she was not thrilled. I introduced Captain Kev and Miniature Mike, a crusty old captain with his very short, wild and crazy sidekick.

Here is an excerpt from *The Black Widow Trainer* that describes what it was like when Misty met Captain Kev and Miniature Mike:

Standing before Misty grinning, was a middle-aged man with a handsome, weather-worn face and short-cropped salt-and-pepper hair. He wore a patch over his left eye, but the other was sparkling blue and looked at her intensely, as if it was looking for the other eye as well. She could tell from the file pictures that it was Captain Kev.

Misty felt a pair of strong arms clench around her waist and a face pressed itself between her breasts and felt her hands pinned at her side. Looking down in confusion, she saw a boyish face framed in floppy brown hair and a pair of burning brown eyes looking up at her.

"Uh..."

"I'm Michael, said her captor. "Everyone calls me Miniature Mike. You can call me Mikey, or Mike, or even Miniature Mike if you like." He was indeed small, only four foot eight in boots. He showed no signs of letting go, so she smiled at him like one might smile at a toddler latching to one's leg, and wiggled her hands up over his arms and eased him off.

In real life, cousin Kevin is fun-loving and, let's say... outspoken. You always know what's on his mind. Mike is just as fun-loving. He also is wiley strong, very short, and his eyes look twice their size peering from his coke bottle thick glasses. Think Kurt Russell paired with Johnny Depp's character in *Pirates of the Caribbean.*

The Kenai Peninsula gave me the perfect backdrop for their escapades due to its remoteness. Homer at the far tip and Seward provided the seedy bars and seasonal workers who stayed until termination dust — that's the first snow that signals the end of the working season.

I spotted a dry-docked boat with unbelievable character, not to mention the worn condition, which naturally, I used as Captain Kev and Miniature Mike's escape boat. The reader could sense they were in trouble, hiding from the law in Alaska, but Misty didn't catch on until their escape scene.

I remember working through my notes on the flight home, and then, on a weekday, sitting down to write. I didn't stop writing until I had knocked out the entire sixty-page adventure. I never would write unless I was rested and had a plan. What surprised me the most was that all I would have was an outline in my head, and the creative aspect came when I was in the throes of writing. It was like an out-of-body experience with a fiber optic cable connected to the collective consciousness of the universe. The best way I can describe Alaska is the great northwest on steroids.

My friend, Roger Davidson, called one day and suggested traveling to London with him for his consulting trip. He is one of the top supermarket analysts in the world and was meeting with London firms on Fleet Street. I immediately began wondering what the city could inspire in me. My first thoughts were of dark, foggy streets and a sense of espionage and danger. I was all in.

Throughout the book, as Misty was away, her husband, Rob, needed to deal with his feelings. What better way than to have him fall for a barista at the local coffee shop? Of course, being such a nice guy, Rob would never approach her on his own. Amelia would have to make the first move.

I decided to create a character as dark and complex as London itself. I decided Peter, her client in Beaver Creek, would ask Misty a favor. He wanted her to train his identical twin brother in London. It took some convincing, but she finally agreed. I needed to create someone powerfully built, with a balding head, high intensity, and an above-all complex demeanor. Who better than Roger Davidson himself?

My business associates at H-E-B Video Central knew Roger well. He's 6'4", about 220 pounds, and works out regularly. He was pretty much all business and high intensity. Every morning we could hear his big size fourteens walking down the hall as he whistled a tune. But thanks to the close friendship we had made during the video days of the eighties and early nineties, I knew another side.

We would often travel the territory together to visit stores, and Austin, Texas was our favorite stop. That's where Roger introduced me to the margaritas at the Uptown Enchilada Bar. I laughed when mine came out in a tiny glass. But after three, my head was abuzz. Roger added, "Oh, by the way, they use Everclear." I didn't care what they were made of because I felt — as Tony the Tiger says — "Grrrrrrreat!"

The next stop was Sixth Street, the University of Texas bar scene. We parked a block away and walked down a side street. Feeling no pain, Roger stopped to see if he could kick down a parking meter with his foot. That's when I knew there was more to him than met the eye. Roger was the oldest of four boys: Roger, Scott, John, and David. His parents were both legally blind, but that didn't stop them from attending night classes and making the most of it. His dad was strict and full of platitudes. I'm now good friends with his other brothers, and they often say things like; "You're running around here like a blind dog in a meat house!" or, "If you had a brain, you'd take it out and play with it."

When his parents were gone at night and getting an education, Roger had to run the house and play parent to his brothers. He was a grocery sacker and night stocker at H-E-B while he got his degree at UT. I don't think he has ever slowed down since or had time to reflect. I knew Roger would make a perfect Ivan.

Here is an excerpt from the *Black Widow Trainer* with Misty's first encounter with Ivan:

> *Unlike Peter, Ivan showed up promptly at 8:00 AM, not a minute late. Misty noticed that he indeed looked almost exactly like Peter. They seemed to be about the same size and balding, but Ivan had a close-cropped grey beard. Misty*

thought it was a nice touch. I need to talk Peter into growing a beard, she thought.

Also, unlike Peter, there was nothing nonchalant about Ivan. He seemed to measure his every move, and Misty noticed his eyes surveying the entire club as he made his way toward them.

After many weeks of training Ivan and enjoying London, her friend and bodyguard, Miguel, found out his wife cheated on him. Misty assured him she would be okay and sent him home.

Ivan would never let on about what he did for a living, and eventually, the curiosity got the better of her. She put on an overcoat and followed him one dreary night. Misty watched across the street as Ivan talked to some rough-looking men in a restaurant. When they dispersed, she decided to approach Ivan, but it was dark and foggy, and they all went in different directions. Thinking she saw him go down an alley, Misty conjured up the nerve to go after him. Here is another excerpt from *The Black Widow Trainer*:

With her usual enthusiasm and zest, she walked towards the man she thought was Ivan and said, "Ivan, what are you guys doing?"

The large man did not immediately turn around to greet her, so she glanced at the other man. It was at that moment she realized these men were not English. It was impossible to tell where they were from. Dark hair, dark eyes, but fair skin. Just then, the large man turned around and stared down at Misty, noticing the big scar running down the right side of his face. Misty then saw the man lying at the big guy's feet. He lay there writhing in agony while blood dripped out of his mouth. The men weren't sure exactly what to do, so they looked at each other for an answer. Misty's temperature inside her overcoat rose, and she became clammy all over. That's when panic sunk in. Just as the men seemed to resolve what to do next, Misty turned and bolted back up Tavistock Street. She could hear the men's feet pounding the pavement closely behind her. When the men barked out instructions to each other, it became obvious that they were from Eastern Europe.

Misty felt clumsy running in her overcoat, so she began to yank it off, which slowed her pace. One of the men got close just as she pulled free, and she threw the coat in his face, causing him to lose his footing and stumble. It was all Misty needed to put some distance between her and her pursuers as she turned right on Christine Street. They may have been some of the scariest men on the planet, but they were no match for her as a runner. A few may have been able to give her a go in the fifty-yard dash, but none of them had her combination of speed and stamina. She was quickly able to move up the steep grade of Christine Street, adding to her lead.

And so it began. The chase lasted for ten pages or more, eventually ending up in Ivan's room. It took a while, but Ivan finally came clean about being a CIA agent working with Scotland Yard to uncover a Belarus drug cartel. But the better drama was the fearful Misty locked in Ivan's room, not knowing who he was or if she could trust him. The tensions ran high. Eventually...

Panic-stricken, she slowly shimmied her way back up the wall, keeping her eyes fixed on Ivans's face. Misty pushed him aside and ran into the bathroom, slamming the door behind her.

And then the truth about his brother:

"When I'm on special assignment, I'm Ivan, but when I'm waiting for an assignment, I hide my identity as Peter."

Misty pulled herself closer to Ivan's body and looked up at him. "So who are you really, Ivan or Peter?"

Ivan let her loose, walking over to the bed, and sat down heavily. He bent over, put his head in his hands, and started talking. "I have been switching back and forth for so long that I'm not sure anymore."

Misty sensed the anguish in his voice.

So I ended the book with Misty drained from the adrenalin rush and wanting to come home to repair things with Rob. But she found it was too late. It cleared the way for her to relocate to Argentina.

I spent several days walking the same streets of London she ran down. Everything was accurate to the phone booth she hid in and the hotel they stayed in. If someone went to London, they could read the chapters as they walked the same streets.

Captured Prey Cliff Notes

With *The Black Widow Trainer* set to be published, I turned my attention to book two. Having traveled to Alaska and London to research the last adventures of *The Black Widow Trainer*, I decided to tackle my hometown of San Antonio, and all south Texas had to offer.

Misty moved in with Gabriella in Argentina, using it as her base of operations. Because of Misty's harrowing experience in London, Gabriella took control of finding Misty's next client. Gabby wanted to ensure it was a safe choice, but knew Misty would not be thrilled, so she sent Misty and Miguel off on her private jet, destination unknown. The pilot instructed not to say, and Miguel held the particulars in a sealed letter Gabriella had entrusted to him. And for a good reason. Her client was Chester Naples, a toilet manufacturer in San Antonio, Texas. I patterned Chester after an old high school classmate named Chester Maples. If you recall me mentioning it at the beginning of this book, Chester was the kid who resembled Ichabod Crane. Misty detested everything about him.

Chester owned a ranch west of town, and one day at the gym, his Ranch foreman visited Chester. The following is an excerpt from *Captured Prey*:

> *Misty bent over, her hands on her knees, and breathed in deeply as she tried to clear her head.*
>
> *Chester said, "Excuse me for a minute, Misty, I need to spend some time with Travis."*

Curious, Misty lowered herself to a seat on the floor, propped herself up against the wall, and eyed Chester's acquaintance up and down. Travis was ruggedly handsome, with long, dark brown hair pulled into a ponytail. His tight, navy blue short-sleeved shirt exposed a well-developed upper body. Thick rounded shoulders, massive pecs, and triceps so ripped she could make out their V-shaped bulge from a distance. His tight-fitting Wrangler jeans were packed with powerful thighs and anchored by two well-rounded buttocks. The jeans draped over his cowboy boots perfectly.

Misty couldn't wait to find out how this deliciously handsome man fit into the picture. Snapping herself out of her stupor, she popped up off the floor and walked in their direction with her usual confidence and enthusiasm. Travis's dark brown eyes lured Misty towards him, but to her dismay, Chester slapped Travis on the shoulder before she could get there and turned to walk back to the workout machines.

Travis lost his parents at a young age and was raised by his uncle, who was previously the foreman of Chester's ranch. Travis took advantage of the insurance money from his parent's death and graduated from the McCombs School of Business at the University of Texas. He moved to Wall Street and worked for a firm, was about to make partner, and was close to proposing to his girlfriend. Life was good.

But then his girlfriend's parents, who were New York elites, insisted that their daughter would not marry a ranch boy from Texas. Her parents called off the wedding and threatened to take their daughter out of their will. Travis snapped out of his depressed mood when he got word that his uncle, who he admired, had died of a heart attack. Travis grabbed the next flight home, and once back on the ranch, he quit his job.

I decided to develop Travis out of clay. He would be confident yet reserved — the perfect specimen of an independent-thinking man with resolve. And he was reserved when he met Misty due to the two disasters he was trying to digest. For Misty, who was used to getting what she wanted, working her way into his life was to be the most difficult challenge of her life.

Misty comes up with excuses every weekend, faking being sick, among many others, to escape San Antonio and explore the sights and sounds of Texas. But her first trick was to get invited to Chester's ranch. Once there, she found herself isolated in a guest camp.

Bored and disappointed, she takes off down a dirt road leading up to the gate in the sweltering heat. Naive to the dangers in the country and the toll the Texas heat and humidity could make and misjudging the distance, she precariously put herself in trouble. Here is an excerpt from *Captured Prey*:

> *Although hot and thirsty, Misty chose not to dwell on her predicament. Instead, she enjoyed the tranquility of being secluded in the country and let her mind wander at will.*
>
> *She was startled by some rustling in the brush nearby but quickly settled down once she saw the culprit, a cute little piglet that couldn't have been over a month old. Misty walked in its direction, wondering if she could pet it.*
>
> *As soon as she had laid a hand on him, the piglet let out a series of loud squeals. Then, the entire litter came out of the brush not more than twenty yards away. An ugly, two-hundred-pound male razorback emerged from the brush. She instantly fixed her sights on his nine-inch tusks. Immediately in fight-or-flight mode, she chose the latter and bolted.*

Within seconds she was being followed by a ferocious, mean, and pissed-off razorback. Off the main highway and flying through the underbrush, Misty's mind turned to the night the European drug dealers chased her in London. Being in the crosshairs of a snorting and squealing wild boar seemed just as terrifying. Her central nervous system was being put to the test, once again. She briefly looked up from her zigzag course through the brush long enough to spot a ranch house not too far ahead. She set a course for the front door. Her lungs burning and her throat parched, Misty felt like she was running through a blast furnace in a hundred-degree heat. Too frightened to look back, she concentrated on dodging the small brush and cactus plants in her path. But when the seriousness of the situation sunk in, Misty began wondering if she could make the house before being overtaken by the beast.

It felt like it was only a matter of time before the horrible creature on her tail struck her down, but just as she was about to give up, she heard a voice in the distance yelling, "Jump into the water tank-now!"

When she located where the voice was coming from, she saw a man pointing to a round water tank underneath an old windmill. It sat to her left, only thirty feet away. Misty attempted to change directions on the fly. As she did, the razorback clipped her trailing leg, causing her to fall. The pain from the cactus plant was excruciating. Luckily, a rush of adrenalin shot through her, and she sprang to her feet.

Misty reached her target and flung herself over the side, seconds before the boar rammed into the side of the tank. Now totally submerged in water, she lay motionless at the bottom. Exhausted and afraid, the pleasant feeling of cool water on her overheated body kept her at the bottom until her burning lungs cried out for air. She exploded to the surface, sucking in hot South Texas air until her breathing returned to normal. Just as she was regaining her composure, Misty was shocked by the sound of a big splash behind her.

In her current state of mind, Misty found it challenging to discern fact from fiction. She felt something grab her by the arms and let out a scream. She found herself in the arms of a man who was naked from the waist up. The man's dripping wet, tanned upper torso glistened in the sunlight. His ruggedly handsome face reminded her of the Marlboro Man. After shading her eyes, she realized it was Travis. Having traveled to the ranch expressly to run into him, she was now in his arms with his full, undivided attention. She couldn't have planned it any better if she tried.

And so they meet. To those who don't live in Texas, that sequence may have felt exotic. To those of us who grew up there, it not only seems perfectly normal, but we may have experienced something similar. Like when my good friend, Greg Smith, began shooting at a pack of hogs with a twenty-two pistol, riling them up! I ran lickety-split back to the ranch house.

The courting to come has many challenges. First, Misty gets Travis to take her country dancing. Here is a scene from *Captured Prey* that takes place at Gruene Hall, north of New Braunfels on the Guadalupe River. I was built in 1878, and not much has physically changed. It still has open-air dancing — home to new talents like George Strait, Hal Ketchum, and Lyle Lovett through the years. Too many to list. And John Travolta's famous dance scene in the movie *Michael*.

Three beers later, Misty found herself sitting alone while Travis visited the men's room. By now, her sweat-soaked La

Perla lingerie clung to her body. Her brow was shining with beads of sweat. Sleeveless, she used the hem of her skirt to wipe her forehead. As she bent over, the blood rushed to her head and left her grasping for support. She leaned against the wall to keep the room from spinning. She got a short respite from the heat when a heavenly gust of wind blew through the chicken wire. When the breeze subsided, she succumbed to the elements once again.

I often would drive back to places I already knew to ensure I got the layout right in my head. Other points of interest were Mustang Island near Corpus Christi, where Misty reluctantly went with friends to get over the fact that Chester told Travis he would fire him if he ever went out with Misty again. Misty goes partying on Sixth Street in Austin, where she attempts to ride a mechanical bull, and partying on a boat in the cove on Travis' lake. There are good descriptions of famous hotels in Austin and San Antonio along with the Alamo, among others.

In this excerpt from *Captured Prey*, Travis struggles with Chester's mandate, and his best friend tries to talk him into calling Misty.

Travis walked over to the chair opposite Blake, removed his boots, and settled in.

"Okay Blake, let's get this over with. What's on your mind?"

"I want to know why you didn't show up at Gruene Hall with Misty Tuesday night, and why you haven't been returning my phone calls."

Travis took several gulps of his tea, set the glass on the table, and locked eyes with Blake. "Mr. Naples told me in no uncertain terms that if I continued to see Misty, he would fire me. There, are you happy?"

"It doesn't matter if I'm happy. The only thing that matters is whether you're happy, and it's obvious you're not."

Travis leaned back, placing his hands behind his head. Blake let some time pass before continuing. "Okay, so Mr. Naples is an asshole. What else is new? All I know is that Saturday night at Gruene Hall, you were the old Travis. This girl's the best thing that's happened to you since your uncle passed away. Misty's a godsend, man. She's the antidote for your misery."

Travis still didn't answer, but Blake kept pushing forward. "Screw your job, man! You have a business degree. You were on your way to making a partner at a prestigious firm before the sky fell in on you. What the heck are you afraid of? Go get her, man!"

Blake knew it was time to back away and let things sink in, so he stood up to leave. As he walked past Travis on his way to the door, Travis reached out and grabbed his arm, and gave it a gentle squeeze to let him know he appreciated his concern.

Ultimately Travis stands up to Chester, and Chester sends Misty back to Argentina. Travis winds up taking his old job back in New York. So my experiment with writing romance comes to a close. Next up, Washington DC, with side trips to New York. I packed my bags and took a trip to see Roger, who lives just south of DC, and joined him on a consulting trip to New York to do my research. Time to see how much trouble we can get Misty into next. Romance time is over, for now.

Henry is a sitting US Congressman from the state of Alabama.

He had a comfortable lead in the polls eleven months before election day. His campaign manager, Rick, has informed him he has a new contender. Rick had run an internal poll, and she was only ten points back. Molly, the sitting Attorney General in Henry's home state of Alabama, was Miss Alabama and polling well with women. Here's some of their conversation from *Captured Prey*:

> Rick took a picture down from the wall and placed it in front of him.
>
> Henry looked puzzled. What does my college football picture have to do with anything?"
>
> "You were a pretty good-looking guy yourself at one time." "What do you mean at one time?"
>
> There you go, Henry. You know you've still got it. A little bodywork and we can start herding some of those women's votes back into our camp!"
>
> Henry sat back with his arms behind his head. Rick knew that was the posture he always took before giving in. "I guess I could lose twenty pounds if I had a personal trainer."
>
> Rick grinned. "Not just any personal trainer. A Black Widow Trainer."
>
> "Black Widow Trainer? What the hell does that mean?"

A cab pulls up to the Sixth Circuit Court in Alabama. The high-powered campaign manager gets out. She meets with Melanie, Molly's assistant who attended college with Cindy, the new campaign manager, and convinces Cindy to take the job. The following excerpt is from *Captured Prey*:

"So tell me about Molly, so I know what I'm getting myself into."

Melanie scrunched her nose. "You, my friend, are going to earn your money. Molly is ruthless. I've tried to handle her, but I'm not having an easy go of it. She's smart as can be, but she's inexperienced when it comes to national politics. Couple that with her hardheadedness, and I'm about ready to pull out my hair.

"Sounds like just another prima donna politician to me. Don't worry; I can handle her. Anything else?"

"Top in her class, strong-minded, and aggressive, but is a popular district attorney. They love how tough she has been on crime, so she's not just another pretty face."

"Nice!" said Cindy. "How's she doing in the polls?"

"Our internal polling has her leapfrogging the other contenders but still around 8 points behind Henry." Melanie gushed.

Cindy looked stunned. "Wow! I had no idea. We can make a name for ourselves if Molly closes that gap."

Cindy delivers the news about Henry's new trainer.

"Find out everything you can about Henry's trainer," Molly said to Cindy. "Who she is, where she's from, and who she'd been training. Hire a private investigator. I know plenty, but I'd prefer we use someone who can't be traced back to me."

Henry's manager, Rick, heard gossip about Henry's new

trainer's beauty and persona. When Rick said he would take care of the money, he took it from Henry's campaign funds. Henry didn't know. Rick tells Henry about the image problem, and they decide to train at night in the basement gym of an old friend who is out of the country.

Molly and Cindy have a meeting with their hired private eyes. Real shady characters. They have done background checks on Misty and the clients she's trained. DC private dicks have their advantages. The following excerpt is from *Captured Prey*:

> "This Misty dame is referred to as the 'Black Widow Trainer' in certain circles. She hires out to wealthy individuals for three months at a time. We hear that sometimes the client makes it through the three months of training, and sometimes they don't. Either way, she gets paid in full."

> "This gal gets top dollar," he continued, "she gets to choose from over hundreds of applicants. The guys that get selected feel as if they just won the lottery. The fact that someone from DC was selected this time around seemed to give the guys something to talk about, resulting in easy access to the information."

When they tell them how much money Misty makes, Molly knows Henry's wife well enough to be confident he could not hide it from personal funds. They have trouble tracking down any of her old clients. Captain Kev and Miniature Mike are in the wind, Ivan is untraceable, and Gabriella keeps things close to the vest. But her last client, Chester, seems like an easy target. They dispatch the boys to San Antonio to see what they can dig up.

Misty calls Travis in New York and asks him if she can come to visit this weekend. He seemed pleased and told her to catch a train. They have a great time. In this excerpt from *Captured Prey*, it is later that night. Travis is cooking Misty dinner when the doorbell rings.

"My hands are gross," said Travis. "You mind seeing who it is?"

Misty took another sip of her wine, slid off the counter, and headed toward the door. The doorbell rang again before she could arrive.

"Hold your horses, I'm coming," she said under her breath.

She swung the door wide open. In front of her stood a well-dressed lady with a look on her face that said, Who the hell are you!

Misty wondered the same. She was moderately pretty with stylish short brown hair, hazel eyes, a cute button nose, and a lean body.

Rich bitch, for sure, Misty thought after noticing her expensive jewelry.

Once the women inspected each other thoroughly, the woman demanded, "Who are you?"

You can imagine where this goes from here: downhill. Travis didn't expect Emily, the old girlfriend that he started dating again to get his life back to normal. Emily was supposed to be at her folk's house on Long Island, so Travis didn't say anything to Misty. She could tell he was stumbling and lying, so she went along with it to the point that Emily asked Misty if she was staying at the hotel around the corner. Misty said yes, picking up her coat and heading out.

After clearing Emily's interrogation, Travis called Misty, but she didn't pick up. He sent her text after text, saying he was just a dumb cowboy and taking all the blame. Misty finally texted back and said, "I'm coming, but you've got some explaining to do." After the truth, lots of apologies, and somewhat of a reconciliation, Misty takes the train back to DC in the morning. They both knew they needed time to sort things out. But it was obvious who Travis preferred, yet Emily's nasty breakup could have been detrimental to his career.

The two brother private detectives flew to Texas to meet with Chester, who was, at first, obstinate. The brothers were Hispanic but adopted by a well-connected Italian family. While at dinner, Cindy calls them with some information she dug up on Chester. It had to do with flying hookers from Vegas over the state line to have sex with a contingent of Japanese businessmen on his ranch. They squeezed him until he gave them the confidential contract Misty made him sign to train him.

I got myself trapped in my storyline and stopped writing for a few days until I realized a scene that was already in the Texas chapters could be used to squeeze Chester. I was thrilled when I figured it out. That kind of thing can happen if you don't have a full outline of where you are going and figure the story out along the way. But that's how I write.

So Travis starts texting Misty, saying he's thinking of breaking up with Emily due to how she treated Misty and how sorry he felt. In a coded sort of way, he asked Misty to come back to New York to help him think it through. Misty smiles. But Misty had also gotten a call from Chester's wife, who she had gotten to know well in Texas, letting Misty know Chester had given the confidential contract to two individuals that the local district attorney's office had asked Chester to meet. After spending the afternoon re-reading her contract with Henry, she realized there was damaging information to Henry if it got out.

Meanwhile, Molly is meeting with her paralegals in this excerpt from *Captured Prey*:

> *"You can start with the Mann Act," said Milly. "After that, search for any laws that pertain to using campaign funds or public funds for personal use if you are in office."*

Misty decides to tell Henry about the contract, and Henry calls Rick to meet. After a bit, Rick asks Henry to let him think about things.

> *"Fine," said Henry. When Rick was almost to the door, the congressman spoke again. "Maybe you should tell me first. Where did you get the funds to pay Misty?"*
>
> *Rick came to a complete stop.*
>
> *"You've never questioned where I got the money before. Are you sure it's a good idea to start now?"*
>
> *"I never asked before because having to explain it to the FBI was never a high probability."*
>
> *Rick walked back to Henry. "Remember, you didn't want to use personal funds, so I had no choice but to dip into your campaign funds."*
>
> *"I see," said Henry. He then placed his hand on Ricks'*

shoulder. *"It doesn't matter a rat's ass whose fault it is. We are both culpable."*

Henry is smart enough to lie about needing to do something for the next ten days, and he would like Misty to go back to New York for a while. He needed to keep a low profile, and the last thing he wanted was to be seen with Misty. Misty uses the time to put her relationship with Travis back together.

In this excerpt from *Captured Prey*, Molly and Cindy are meeting. Molly is speaking.

> *"One option is to provide the US Attorney General's office with enough information to charge Henry under the Mann Act. All we have to do is prove he slept with a prostitute."*

> *Cindy says, "I suggest we give the US Attorney General's office enough information to open an investigation. You and I both know Henry didn't use personal funds to pay for Misty's services, so they likely move onto investigating Henry's campaign finances. Willfully converting money from a political action committee for personal use is a federal crime."*

> *"In* Caminetti v. the United States, *the judge ruled that a non-commercial consensual sexual liaison — consensual extramarital sex, in other words — falls within the genre of "immoral sex" and is enough to bring charges."*

> *Cindy said, "So the key is to get Misty to admit having sex with Henry, whether we can prove he paid for it or not."*

Molly's personal friend is an investigative reporter for the *Washington Post*. She will ask her to leak it to the government. The FBI picks up Misty later in New York and brings her to an interrogation room. Misty won't talk. They drum up a bogus "false swearing" charge so they can keep her in the cell overnight to soften her up. Misty is placed in a cell with a badass Amazonian-looking woman egged on by the cellmates across the hall. This excerpt from *Captured Prey* includes the ending of a long, drawn out fight. Misty refused to fight until she had no choice.

> *"Misty exploded through her target with such force that Sosa slammed into the back wall of the cell. The horrifying thud Misty's right shoulder made as it drove into Sosa's chest was remarkably similar to that of a heavyweight fighter's fist making contact with his opponent's body. Sosa dropped to the floor, thrashing around like a freshly caught fish in the bottom of a boat. Misty stood over her and watched her curl up into a ball. She waited until Sosa's breathing returned to normal before she leaned over and wrapped her opponent's hair tightly around her right hand. This time it was Misty's turn to pull Sosa's head back by the hair and look into her eyes.*
>
> *"I'd make you my bitch if you weren't so damn ugly," said Misty.*

Ivan has been secretly keeping an eye on Misty while stationed in Langley, stateside. He wanted to meet her in public. In *The Black Widow Trainer*, they had gone to see *The Phantom of the Opera*. She receives a single ticket to that night's New York showing. She has her suspicions and goes. Feeling she has made a mistake after the show begins, she contemplates leaving. But Ivan shows. Ivan will be a key component in helping Misty through her ordeal.

Molly meets Misty in a bar in New York and tells Misty that Chester will swear Travis (as the foreman) was responsible for hiring the hookers for the Japanese businessmen unless Misty testifies against Henry. Molly tells Misty she can work a plea bargain for herself. All the Attorney General's office wants is to take down a sitting member of Congress. Molly tells Misty to meet her at a specific restaurant in DC at noon on Friday. But she has to decide by then.

Misty knows that if she takes down a client, much less a congressman, the news will travel the world in hours. Her career as the Black Widow Trainer will be over. And if she doesn't, dear Travis' career will be over.

I'm not going to spoil the ending. But I will give you a clue in this excerpt from *Captured Prey*:

> "*The fresh March air invigorated Misty on her walk back to the Hampton Hotel . She felt alive for the first time in days. Walking past the White House on her way, she noticed the tender green buds forming on the cherry trees, realizing the coming of spring would be rejuvenating.*"

Hanging by a Thread Cliff Notes

We go back to Argentina to begin book three. Gabriella's bodyguard, Tom, drives Misty back from Buenos Aires abreast the Rio de la Plata coastline to Gabriella's mansion along the Atlantic Ocean. Misty sees a ragged old steamboat that looks just like the one Captain Kev and Miniature Mike used to escape Alaska. They knew Misty lived around Buenos Aires, and for lack of a better idea of where to lay low, they decided to go there. However, it took them over a year with stops to repair their boat along the way. Tom follows the Captain until he docks.

I decided to provide Misty with a female antagonist. In this excerpt from *Hanging by a Thread*, Misty's bodyguard, Miguel, is recuperating from an injury. Tom's son, a powerfully built kid in his early twenties named Thor, begs to take Miguel's place on their next escapade.

> Someone behind them said, "My, my, my. What a strapping young man!"

> Misty turned around to see a woman emerging from the deck below. She had gorgeous, silky, jet-black hair that hung down to the middle of her back. She glanced confidently at Misty. Lush eyebrows that seemed even darker than her hair framed her catlike greenish-blue eyes. The woman turned her head and set course for Thor. From her firm, protruding butt anchored by muscled thighs to her powerfully built arms, her body was exquisite in every way. Although she was strong, she looked more like a finely honed athlete than a weight

lifter. Her movements were as agile as a gazelle with ample breasts laying heavy on her chest. Misty looked down at her own body and back to the women.

"Ugh, Misty, I would like to introduce you to Monique," said the Captain. When neither responded, he added, "Monique, this is Misty." Misty extended her hand, and Monique gripped it firmly. Each made the other aware of her full strength.

Captain Kev and Miniature Mike drop anchor in front of Gabriella's villa, high above the sea. One evening while the women are out for a swim in Gabby's pool, they see a terrible explosion. The women are devastated and hold a funeral without body parts. The following day, two strange-looking men screech up to the front of Gabriella's house, where the women are standing and exit the vehicle. The following is an excerpt from *Hanging by a Thread*:

Miniature Mike tipped the brim of his sombrero up enough for Misty to recognize him. His grin was wide as the fake handlebar mustache he was wearing. A prosthetic right arm confirmed that the man was Captain Kev, brown shoe polish was applied generously to their faces.

After they located Sam, the man who was going to run their new bar under his name, Captain Kev and Miniature Mike staged their deaths in hopes of disappearing to St. Thomas. Don't worry, we'll get there later in the story. But Roger and I will get there first so I can research the Caribbean.

Misty's new client is the owner of a large casino in Vegas. I had been to Vegas at least twenty-five times previously, primarily to attend the VSDA (video show) and CES (electronics show). I decided to visit again. I felt it would set the mood for the following chapters. Here are some passages from *Hanging by a Thread* that describe the appearance of the new client, Salvatore, and demonstrate Misty's continued frustration with Monique:

> *Misty prepared herself for a man with a healthy ego. A large floor poster depicting a middle-aged man trying to look cool stood to the left of the entrance. A throwback to the seventies, he had left his shirt unbuttoned almost down to his naval. A massive gold chain hung around his neck, resting atop a carpet of thick, black chest hair comfortably. His index finger and thumb pointed at you as if mimicking a gun. The line "I'm The Guy. Who are you?" ran along the bottom edge of the poster.*

> *Misty extended her hand to greet him, but she quickly dropped it when she realized he was looking past her. He brushed past Misty on his way to Monique. He took Monique's hands and kissed each side of her cheeks, which Monique enjoyed very much.*

> *"Magnificent!" he said. "It's obvious why they refer to you as the Black Widow Trainer."*

In this excerpt of *Hanging by a Thread*, you'll see that Salvador had plenty of goons working for him:

> *Misty and Thor were halfway down the passageway that led to their elevator when they spotted Antonio and his men leaning against the wall. As Misty and Thor approached, Antonio stepped into the middle of the hall to block them from passing.*

> *"Isn't it a little past your bedtime?" Antonio said.*

Turned off by the tone and the alcohol on his breath, Misty said calmly, "I'm exhausted, Antonio. Please move out of my way."

The rest of the men moved off the wall and took a position behind Antonio. Thor stepped between Misty and Antonio.

Gary owns a small casino named Devil's Cove. His casino is not for sale when Salvador purchases the city block. Salvador had to leave it standing while building his massive casino. Devil's Cove took up a small section of the far right corner of the casino. Customers had to go in and out through the front, as Gary and Salvador's relationship was contentious. The real-life Gary that I patterned the character after is my good friend, Gary Ross. I got to know him on the National Board of VSDA. From *Hanging by a Thread*, here is Misty's first impression of Gary:

A man standing behind Misty said, "Aren't you going to place a bet?"

Misty looked him over. He seemed to be in his fifties, around six feet tall and 180 pounds. She was attracted to his semi-long, dusty-blonde hair and boyish good looks.

Gary invites Misty to his cabin in the nearby Sierra Nevada Mountain range, when Salvador takes an unscheduled trip to Sicily for a family emergency. In real life, when I was in Vegas for our big VSDA convention with the entire Video Central management team, I took a trip to camp out on the ledge of the Grand Canyon with Greg Smith and Alan Market. I had never paid any attention to the mountains to the west of Vegas. But I noticed them as we passed through on the way to the North Rim.

While there, Gary tells Misty some very confidential information about the FBI investigation of Salvador for a murder. Misty has also gotten to know Escobar, her massage therapist who is available to her per her contract. Escobar is Cuban. He is in America illegally and at the mercy of Salvador. He knows more than he should, and he tells Misty more than he should about Salvador. Escobar is trying to earn enough money to go back to Cuba and propose to the girl he loves.

In this scene from *Hanging by a Thread*, you'll learn Monique's backstory. She revisits a strip joint that has meaning to her past. We begin with her making her way to the back looking for something.

> *Monique stood quietly outside the open door, watching Mr. Montoya busily doing paperwork. His grey hair made him look a bit older, but his facial features were the same. She had worked under him in servitude for two long years, but she had no ill-feeling toward him: she knew he had no choice but to obey his bosses' orders. He had never mistreated her while she worked for him, and she gave him credit for that. But that was all the credit she would give him.*
>
> *"Who are you?" he demanded when he noticed her standing in the doorway. "What do you want?"*
>
> *Monique walked confidently toward him, placed her hands in the middle of his desk, and leaned in until their faces were only inches apart. "I was your personal property for two long years, and you don't recognize me?*
>
> *He sat back and diligently studied her, eyebrows furrowed; Monique stepped back, placing her hands on her hips."*

His eyes opened wide as he said with trepidation, "Monique, honey. How have you been, how is your —"

"How's my father?"

"Yes, I can see you still harbor ill feelings toward him."

"Why wouldn't I? He sold me into servitude to pay his gambling debts. How much was a little slave girl worth back then?"

Mr. Montoya stood to his feet in reverence. "I had little choice, honey. You know I don't own this place. I just run it for some real unsavory men. Your dad owed them a mountain of money, and had we not worked out a deal, they most likely would have killed him." With a nervous smile, he added, "You wouldn't have wanted your poor father dead, would you?"

"Wanted him dead? Hell, I probably would have pulled the trigger. So how much, Montoya?

"How much was a sixteen-year-old virgin pole dancer worth?" Mr. Montoya lowered his head and said in a soft voice, "Two hundred thousand dollars."

"Two hundred thousand dollars?"

"One hundred and fifty thousand to settle his debts, but then he borrowed and lost another fifty thousand, so we kept you another six months." Mr. Montoya smiled feebly.

"I showed off my tits and ass to those filthy men for an extra six months just so my father could blow another fifty thousand dollars gambling."

"Before you get too down on your father, you should know he borrowed the extra fifty to try and win your freedom sooner."

"What an idiot! How long did it take him to lose it?"

"Not long, dear, you know your father was a lousy gambler."

While Salvador was away, Gary had coached Misty up on gambling tendencies, and she took the house for two hundred thousand. Salvador was livid and wanted to pay Gary back. They had learned Gary was going to his cabin for a long weekend, and no one lived within five miles of him. Salvador sends his boys to Gary's cabin ahead to lay in wait. Monique has been shacking up with Salvador all these weeks. She overhears the plan. Her conscience compels her to contact Gary with what she knows (Monique is beginning to develop a little bit of a conscience). Gary's cabin is so remote that there is no cell service until you get near his cabin. Monique leaves him a ton of messages in this excerpt from *Hanging by a Thread*:

When the paved road turned to dirt, Gary noticed fresh vehicle tracks. He assumed the propane man had made them while making his weekly rounds. But when the tracks disappeared before reaching the cabin, he stopped the car in the middle of the road. Just as he reached for the door handle, his cell phone beeped, and the messages he had missed while out of cell service began to blow up his phone. Most of the messages were updates from his casino managers, but one was from a number he didn't recognize. He sat dumbfounded as he listened to the woman's warning.

His mind raced as he thought about his plan of action. Should he go back down the mountain and check on Misty? Or should he deal with the issue at hand? Gary's ancestors were tough and rugged pioneers who had to endure all types of hardships. Up until recently he had lived the good life — that is until Salvatore showed up. Down deep, he had known this day was coming, the day of reckoning. Gary had two choices, turn and run, or face it head-on the way his great-grandfather would have.

As Gary traversed the old hunting trail on the side of the mountain, dusk closed in around him. In the dimming light, he could barely make out the initials carved into the mountain cedar. JD stood for Janet Dewey, his junior high sweetheart. He came upon his childhood fort. The fallen tree branches stacked together, protecting the entrance to the tiny cave. Gary had spent many afternoons crouched behind the earthy wall, BB gun at the ready, shots flying at anything that rustled, such as approaching Indians — whooping and hollering they came, like, well, wild Indians. His heart pounded with every attack. Maybe it was the ghosts of an imaginary Indian he now heard in the windswept valley below. He made a mental note that his fort might be a good place to hide out if things went astray. The terrain soon leveled out, allowing him to quicken his pace. He sat only yards from the house, contemplating his next move. A barn owl hooted, and he remembered the old passageway under the house that his great grandfather had built in the event of an actual Indian attack. He ground his teeth and moved on.

The passageway that led him underneath the master bedroom closet was narrower than he remembered. One by one, he quietly removed the rough-edged floorboard planks until the opening was wide enough for him to pull himself up into the tiny closet. He tiptoed across the bedroom and cracked open the door, thankful he was a stickler about keeping the door hinges well lubricated. His eyes focused on a familiar figure at the end of the hallway. Santo, the one who had roughed him up the first time he told Salvador he would never sell out. Santo's fist had felt like an anvil every time he buried it deep into Gary's gut. His thoughts ran to sweet vengeance. It was time for payback!

The closet was dark, but the blackness didn't stop Gary from locating the leather case he was looking for on the top shelf. It was as heavy as he remembered. He had thought about locking the bedroom door earlier, but he couldn't risk making noise and giving his position away. Any false move and Santo would barrel through the door and give him another beat down. From the look of the club Santo had been holding, it would be far worse than the last time. He meticulously worked the zipper until the case was open. Gary smiled as he felt the contents inside. The last time it was open was five years ago when his now-deceased father had taught him how to fire the prized possession, his great-grandfather's 1875 model Sharps Buffalo rifle. He found the box of ammunition on the middle shelf. There was no mistaking the two-and-a-half-inch 64-millimeter casings he held in his hand. The box was full; there were plenty of rounds for the task ahead. It was time!

Gary had a bounce in his step as he strolled off down the main road to his car. He convinced himself this was for Misty as much as it was for him. There was a slight chill in the air, which only made him feel alive, and he wondered if this was how his ancestors felt when they faced their many challenges. Gary was proud to be carrying their DNA. When he reached the car, he placed the weapon in the backseat and casually got in. He rolled down the windows to enjoy the cool evening air while he listened to the sound of the tires grinding on the gravel road as the Jag rolled back down the mountain.

When he came upon the tire tracks he had noticed earlier, Gary turned off the road. He found his target on the other side of the brush thicket and brought the car to a halt. Gary got out of the car, opened the back door, and pulled out the instrument his ancestors had used to bring down charging buffalo. A single bullet to the beast's onrushing skull and it would crumple to the ground, or so the old stories told. They used black powder ammunition in those days. The smokeless powder ammunition he held in his hand gave the gun over a thousand more foot-pounds of force. He loaded a round in the chamber, locked the gun, and aimed it at the object. Antonio's prize possession, a two hundred thousand dollar gold-colored Maybach, shone like a massive gold nugget from the illumination of the Jag's halogen headlights. Gary let out a chuckle and squeezed off the round. The car was so airtight, not only did the front and rear windows blow out, but the side windows as well. The roar of his gun subsided in time to hear the tinkling of broken glass falling all about.

Santo leaped up and ran to the window. Antonio and Tomasso followed close behind. "What the heck was that?" Tomasso asked. Antonio raised his hand so the boys would be quiet as he trained his ears on a potential subsequent blast.

Gary chambered a second round, curious what sound a 550-grain bullet would make when striking the engine block head-on. The front grill exploded high into the air as the sound echoed through the valley. The loud thud of the grill falling to the ground accompanied by the sound of grinding metal, while the car rocked back and forth as if broadsided by a charging buffalo. Two down and one to go, Gary thought. He threw round after round into his target. He squatted down and took both front tires out with a single round. He then climbed a small hill and aimed at the middle of the undamaged trunk. Gary lay prone on his back as he looked up at the fireball cascading into the sky. The Maybach's rear end lifted high into the air and slammed back to the ground. As he watched the flames, he laughed and thought, Oops, I guess I hit the gas tank.

Salvatore's boys bolted outside the cabin and stared at the fireball in the sky. Antonio cried out in anguish, "Mother Fucker! That's where we parked my car!"

A lot goes on to close out the Vegas chapters. Miguel heals up, and Gabriella, knowing the tough situation Misty is in, sends both Miguel and her bodyguard, Tom, to Vegas. Salvatore discovers Monique was the one who warned Gary. He roughs Monique up and locks her in her bedroom of his hotel suite. Gary convinces Misty she needs to not only leave but get back to the safety of Argentina, as Salvatore is no man to cross.

Misty, Gary, and Gabby hatch a plan. Gary will call Salvatore to his office under the pretense of telling him he's ready to sell Devil's Cove. That will buy them time to get up to Salvatore's quarters at the top of the hotel. Escobar knows he might get in trouble as well, so he gives Miguel the code to Salvatore's private elevator if they will take him with them.

Gary is waiting in his office stalling Salvatore until Misty calls to tell him she is safe in her room. But Misty is grabbed by Antonio's boys, who take her to Salvatore's quarters, where they are holding Monique. Gary continues to stall Salvatore, waiting for the call. Miguel, Tom, and Thor can't find Misty but have no choice but to attempt to break out Monique without knowing if Misty is there as well. A knockdown, drag-out fight ensues. In this excerpt from *Hanging by a Thread*, the fight ends like this:

Across the room, Antonio backed away from Miguel until he was up against the back wall.

With nowhere to go, Antonio said to Miguel in a threatening voice, "You don't know what you are getting yourself into"

"He must think he's THE GUY," Tom yelled out to Miguel in a sarcastic tone.

Antonio pointed his finger at Tom and repeated his threat. Miguel slammed a thunderous fist into Antonio's right shoulder. Antonio's right arm dangled limply by his side as he slid down the wall onto the floor. He sat there, holding his shoulder with his left hand.

"Looking up at Miguel, Antonio said, "Take Misty and get the hell out of here, but remember, there will be a heavy price to pay."

Tom motioned to Misty to follow him toward the door, but Miguel and Thor didn't budge. Tom looked back with a puzzled look. "Aren't you forgetting why we came here?" Thor asked. "Where's Monique?"

Thor walked over to the bedroom door to find it locked. Antonio yelled out, "You better not go in there."

Thor threw his shoulder into the door. The top hinge cracked. Tom motioned for Thor to step back, and Tom rammed into the door knocking it entirely off its hinges. Miguel pushed past them and kneeled by Monique's side. She looked up at him and attempted to grin, but it quickly turned into a grimace. Miguel delicately stroked her long, beautiful black hair. He leaned down and whispered into her ear, "Let me *help you up. It's time to go home."*

Thor walked to her other side and helped Miguel lift her gently off the floor. Almost to the front door, Monique heard Antonio say, "Go ahead and run off but know this, I'll eventually track you down and make you pay.

Monique's brows furrowed. She removed her arms from the boys, pushing them aside, and walked gingerly over to Antonio. With a look of disdain, she said, "Say that again."

"I said —"

Monique's foot crashed into his scrotum before he could finish his sentence. Antonio rolled onto the floor and lay there on top of his bad shoulder in agony. He moaned as Monique made her way to the bedroom, returning with the pillow and blanket she threw on top of Antonio.

"You're probably going to be there for a while, so you might as well be comfortable." Monique placed her arms around the boys again and said, 'Okay, now I'm ready to go."

The plane Gabriella sent them was at the private airport when they got there. Salvatore called in a favor from a friend working at the FAA, and got their tail number. Misty's crew notified them they were being followed. Gabriella is monitoring the situation, calls in a favor, and gets permission to land in Cuba. That would hopefully buy them time to lay low and select a different destination.

I was off to St. Thomas with Roger to get the feel of the land. Blackbeard's Castle, built in 1679, inspired the closing scenes and storyline. It's not what you think. More of a turret, straight up with many floors along the way. Each with slits in the walls for shooting. The top made an excellent lookout post, overseeing only cruise ships these days. I was sure Misty, and her merry men could hang out in Cuba until I got my research done. Red Hook Bay, on the opposite side of the island, proved helpful to visualize Captain Kev's and Miniature Mike's new bar. The one to be under Sam's name.

Misty reunites with Captain Kev and Miniature Mike while getting to know Sam. I came up with Sam myself. I wanted someone with a tragic past who stays within himself. I used the image and voice of Sam Elliott to guide me.

Miguel and Monique are getting close, although she doesn't give in and pushes back in the beginning. Miguel takes her on the ferry to St. John's, where Monique surprises him by taking him to lunch at a place she's very familiar with. Big Momma gives Monique a big hug and cooks up Caribbean food. Monique tells him how Sam had saved her from being robbed and then invited her to travel to the Caribbean with him. Big Mama took care of Monique until she ran into Captain Kev.

Captain Kev talks Misty, Miguel, and Monica into going to an uncharted island to hunt for treasure. They have an old treasure map they acquired, believing it is real. Here's a bit from *Hanging by a Thread* about them heading out:

> *Misty walked the length of the eighty-foot schooner, giving it a thorough inspection. The boat was old and needed repair, but she wouldn't expect anything more from Captain Kev. It was a significant improvement over the Dirty Pirates they sailed out of Alaska in. Her inspection of the compartments below the deck revealed extensive use of quality teak wood. She realized the schooner must have been something special*

in her day. Misty climbed back on deck in time to watch Mikey hoist a Greek Flag. Captain Kev was only a few yards away. "Greek registry, CK?" she yelled.

"Long story," he said with a mischievous grin. "It's probably best you don't know."

Miguel spent the next half hour helping Sam bring a week's worth of provisions aboard. When the galley was fully stocked, Sam returned topside and announced he was heading back to the bar.

They relied on their powerful diesel engine to get them out of the harbor, but once at sea, Captain Kev yelled out, "Mikey and Monique, there's a nice breeze today. Prepare to set sail!" Having done some sailing during her past life in Malibu, Misty helped attach the mainsheet to the forestay and then helped them join the boom to the mast's front."

"Free the shrouds!" the Captain bellowed.

When they finished, Mikey gave the thumbs-up. "Hoist the mast!" Captain Kev shouted, "Let's be on our way," A gust of wind filled the sails, causing the wooden schooner to creak and list slightly to the port side. When it righted itself, they were underway.

Misty made her way to the bow. She hung her arms over the rail and enjoyed the breeze blowing through her hair; she closed her eyes and breathed warm, salty air deep into her lungs. Las Vegas seemed like a distant memory. Now it was time to unwind and get her life back to normal.

Meanwhile, Salvatore finds out where they are and sends

Luigi, a cold-blooded killer, to go with his guys. In this scene from *Hanging by a Thread*, Sally is Sam's latest reclamation project, and he was proud she was making significant progress. And then:

After Sally walked out the back door, Sam carried a tray of clean glasses from the kitchen to the bar. He wondered how Misty and Monique were. His thoughts were interrupted when five men entered. Turning toward them, Sam said, "Sorry, we're closed. Come back at six tonight if it's convenient."

The men made no response. Instead, they dispersed and started to check the place out. Santo walked toward the entrance to the kitchen. Sam stepped in front of him, blocking his path. "I said we're not open." Tomasso leaned against the bar. "We just need some information, and we will be on our way," he said diplomatically.

As Antonio walked onto the back porch, Sam measured the distance between him and the Glock he kept under the bar. Sam stepped out of Santo's path and positioned himself in front of Tomaso to inch his way closer to the weapon without being obvious. Santo moved quickly into the kitchen and began looking around. Luigi walked behind the bar from the opposite end, unknowingly cutting Sam off from his weapon.

"We'd like a little information," Luigi said.

"Sorry, the Tourist and Information Bureau back in town can answer anything you want to know," Sam replied.

"So, do you think they can tell us where Misty is?" Antonio asked as he walked back from the porch. "Or are you the right person to ask?"

"Misty. Sounds like a frozen drink," Sam said. "Maybe you can tell me what's in it."

Santo walked back into the bar from the kitchen and said, "Coast is clear." He opened the door leading to the living quarters and said, "I'll go check it out." Sam worried he would run into Sally.

"We have it from a very reliable source that Misty is staying here," Antonio said.

I hope you didn't tip the guy because he doesn't know what the hell he's talking about."

"We're going to get it out of you one way or another," Luigi said, "Why make it hard on yourself?"

Santo came back in, holding a picture frame in his hand. He held it up for all to see." It looks like you're going to get your bitch back, Antonio," Santo said.

"What about Monique, smart guy?" Antonio asked. "Why don't you tell us where she is! I'll bet Misty won't be far away."

Sam heard the garbage truck pull away and realized he needed to make his move now if he hoped to alert Sally. He turned to Santo, who was close to him, and looked down at his expensive Italian shoes. "You like wearing sissy shoes? I'll bet a C-note you're wearing ladies' panties underneath your trousers."

Santo charged as Sam grabbed a full bottle of whisky and smashed it over his head, stopping him cold. Tomasso and Diego climbed over the bar, positioning themselves on either side of Sam. Sam drove his fist into Diego's solar plexus.

Diego crumpled to the floor like a sack of flour. Tomasso grabbed Sam from behind and dragged him to the floor. Sam reached behind him and placed Tomaso in a chokehold. Sam stopped after Luigi pressed a gun barrel against his temple. Tomasso gagged a few moments after Sam released him. From the corner of his eye, Sam saw Sally standing in the kitchen doorway, scared but unnoticed. She ducked back into the kitchen.

Santo staggered up from the floor and drew his gun. "That son of a bitch busted my skull," Santo said, studying the blood on his fingers. "Let me kill him!"

Luigi pressed his gun barrel into Santo's ribs. "Not yet. He still hasn't told us where Misty is."

Santo and Tomasso each grabbed one of Sam's arms and directed him to a chair. Antonio cut the strings from a guitar left on the stage and tied Sam's hands behind his back. Luigi kneeled on the floor in front of Sam. "It's obvious you are a trained combatant. Navy Seals? Rangers? Special Forces?" Luigi prodded.

When Sam didn't answer, Luigi shook his head and stood up, "Okay, work him over, Santo. If he doesn't give us what we want, kill him."

Sam withdrew into himself as Santo battered him with punches to the head and body. Now and then, the blows would knock Sam and the chair over, but Tomasso and Diego would right him again.

When Santo's hands got sore, he used the leg of a chair to beat Sam around the arms and legs. "You think I'm a sissy now, wise guy," Santo yelled. Luigi stepped between Santo and Sam when he realized Sam was not going to talk. One of Sam's eyes was completely swollen shut, and his face was a bloody mess.

Luigi kneeled, placed his hand under Sam's chin, and raised his head so he could look him in the eyes. "You have one last chance to say something before I let him kill you."

Sam spit some blood on the floor and then smiled the best he could at Luigi. "Special Forces," Sam said proudly.

Luigi dropped his head and looked at the floor. "Got to hand it to you," he said, "you're one tough son of a bitch."

. . .

A group of tourists enters the bar causing them to move Sam to the porch, where he manages to free himself by dropping into the water. He hides out in the water under the living quarters, which are on piers . Sam manages in the dark to reach in his small boat and pull out his scuba gear, moving from place to place under the quarters to escape detection. The men find out what they need to know from Sally. Sam finds her dead in the dumpster in the morning. Misty and the crew are having a high time on the tiny island, looking for gold and exploring the island. Sam takes a boat to Big Mama's house on St John's. He asks Mama:

"Do you still have the chest I left here?"

"Yes, it's up in the attic. I never touched it all dez years."

Sam rose from the chair and laid his ice pack on the table.

211

"Perfect! Tell Jessie I need some explosives. Black powder, if that's all he can find, but C4 would be preferable. Have him visit Mr. Blackwell. He owns a construction company and was a good friend of my father. Tell Blackie it's for Sam, so he knows it will never be traced back to him."

Sam pulled down the old accordion ladder from the ceiling and climbed up into the attic. He found the chest exactly where he had left it ten years ago, right after he had turned in his resignation. He pried the lock open with his pocket knife. First out was his Glock 9-millimeter handgun. He looked down the end of the barrel and made a mental note to clean it before he headed out. A full fifteen rounds were in the first clip but counted only six in the other. He would have to fire it judiciously. The good news was that the Glocks fire even when wet, and he realized that could come in handy on an island. Sam slipped the handgun into the back of his pants and took out his special .357 Python revolver. He loaded six rounds into the cylinder and gave it a spin. If he couldn't shoot around it, he could shoot through it. After stuffing a box of shells into his jacket, he slid the gun into its holster and buckled the belt around his waist.

Next out was his Remington 870 shotgun. The butt was sawed-off to convert it into a pistol grip, and the chamber was modified to hold five rounds instead of three. Sam stood up and placed the rigged parachute cord around his shoulder, and let the rifle hang down across his lower back. He grabbed the gun by the pistol grip, pointed it from his hip, and then let it hang behind his back again. He placed the eight shells in a plastic bag and stuffed them into his jacket pocket. It was then time to clean his guns at the kitchen table while he waited on Jessie, Jr.

The table is set for a raucous time on the tiny island. As you can imagine, Luigi will be there with all the boys. I can promise the action will wear you out, and the levity from Captain Kev and Miniature Mike will give you comic relief. But I'll give you my favorite part before I wind this down. In this excerpt from Hanging by a Thread, Misty and Sam are trapped on top of the fourth floor of a tower similar to Blackbeard's (imagine that). Monique and Miguel have already climbed down the walls with a rope. It was now Misty's turn.

Misty had her head out the window, watching Miguel make his way down the wall when shots rang out. She turned around to the sight of Sam on one knee, holding his left shoulder. He motioned for Misty to stay put, but she ran over to him anyway. Splinters flew into the air all around her from another round of shots. Sam pulled the .357 magnum out of its holster and fired back. The shells penetrated the wooden floor as if made out of balsa wood. The holes were so big, Misty could see through to the next floor below. They heard footsteps running in the other direction. Misty pulled Sam's hand away from his left shoulder. When blood seeped out, she quickly replaced his hand and helped him press it tightly. "Oh, Sam. It looks bad."

"Help me to my feet," he said. "They know our last position, so we need to move."

Sam placed his good arm around Misty's shoulders as she wrapped an arm around his waist. He guided her over to this backpack. "Set me down here."

Misty eased Sam into a sitting position with his back supported by the wall. "I can't leave you now," she said. "You could never make it down that rope in your condition. Give me one of your guns, and I'll help you hold them off."

Sam placed his good hand on the side of Misty's face. "Now, you know I can't let you stay."

Tears streamed down her face.

Sam reached into his vest pocket, took out an old picture, and handed it to Misty. The women in the photo stood arm in arm. One was an older woman, and the other one appeared to be somewhat younger than Misty. She froze when it dawned on her that the younger woman could have been mistaken for her sister.

"My wife and my daughter," he said. "You remind me so much of Sandy. She would have been about your age now."

"My age now, Oh, Sam. Please don't tell me she's dead."

Sam detected noise on the floor below and fired off the remaining three shells from his .357. Miguel yelled out from below, "Hurry up, Misty!"

"Go now!" Sam said as he reloaded the remaining shells into the cylinder of the magnum.

Misty glared into his face. "I'm not leaving until you tell me what happened to your daughter.

Sam sighed. "I was coming back from a mission overseas," he said. "I decided to stay over in Hawaii an extra day. When I got home, the police informed me someone had broken into our home and brutally murdered both my wife, Ginger, and Sandy."

"Oh God, no! I am so sorry!"

Sam looked at her with deep sadness. "If I had only come home when I was supposed to, they would still be alive."

Misty rubbed the tears from her eyes with one hand as she held out the picture for Sam to take. "No, I want you to keep it," he said. "I have no use for it where I'm going. Just promise you will keep it in a safe place." Misty placed her hand inside her shirt, pulled open her bra, and secured it between her bra and her bosom. "It will stay close to my heart, as will you."

Sam patted her arm. "Please, honey. Go now. You don't have much time." She looked over Sam's face, memorizing his every feature. She wiped the tears from her eyes again with her shirtsleeve and then leaned over and kissed Sam on the forehead. She stood up, stepped onto the ledge, and grabbed the rope. Misty looked back to Sam one last time and said, "Give 'em hell, Sammy boy." After which she rappelled down the wall toward an awaiting Miguel. Sam placed the backpack in his lap and prepared for his showdown.

Santo was standing just above Luigi on the ladder leading to the third floor. Santo wanted to impress Luigi by charging to the other side, but Sam's cannon blast from the .357 rounds gave him pause. Antonio, who was still on the first floor, caught a glimpse of Miguel holding the bottom of the rope. "Hey!" he yelled. "They've got a rope and are climbing out the window."

"Well, go outside and shoot the bastard," Luigi yelled back. Antonio ran to the front door and laid his shoulder into it. The jolt sent him to the floor. "They've locked us in," he

yelled. Luigi and Santo gave each other a queer look. "Why would he lock himself inside with us?' Santo asked.

"Shoot at them through the slats in the wall," Luigi yelled back.

When her right foot slipped out from under her, Misty wished she had spent more time on the rock-climbing wall at her gym in Malibu, "Just let yourself down with your arms," Miguel yelled. "You're strong enough."

Miguel heard a gunshot and ducked. The rope became slack in his hands, and a section of it fell onto his head. He looked up and saw Misty hanging by a thread. He could see a gun sticking out of a slit on the second floor. "Swing to the wall and see if you can get a finger hold," Miguel said. "Someone is shooting at you from one of those slits."

After looking down and contemplating jumping, Misty decided to do as Miguel suggested.

Worried that their adversaries would get away, leaving them barricaded in the castle, Luigi placed his gun in the back of Santo's head and said, "Run over to the fourth-floor ladder, or I'll ventilate your brain."

Santo had little doubt Luigi meant what he said, so he rose onto the ladder, stopping just below the door on the floor above. He had no idea Luigi had followed him until he felt a gun pressed in his back. "You're almost there," Luigi whispered.

Santo closed his eyes, clenched his teeth, and pushed the door open. Luigi used the momentum Santo had created to push him up and through the floor from behind. Sam picked up his Glock and put three rounds into Santo's chest. The next two shots rang from Luigi's gun, one penetrating Sam's chest. Sam looked at his chest and then to where the shots came from.

Luigi was on the top step with his gun pointed at him. Sam's Glock fell from his hand onto the floor. Luigi climbed up and strolled over with his gun fixed on Sam's head. He kicked the Glock away and then reached into Sam's holster and removed the .357 magnum.

Luigi held the gun up and looked it over. "I've always thought about getting one of these. I'm sure you won't mind if I keep it." realizing Sam was in desperate straits, he looked out the window. "Well, what do we have here? I guess no castle would be complete without a damsel in distress."

Luigi knew Salvatore wanted Misty alive, but he had other plans. He walked back to Sam and knelt. "Hang on a bit longer, buddy. I wouldn't want to rob you of the opportunity to witness me putting a bullet in your lady friend's head." Sam looked back at Luigi with stone cold eyes.

"I can then place it by your side, the way I placed your other gun by the side of that poor young girl the authorities think you killed back at the bar. I'll just tell Salvatore you went on a shooting spree before I could bring her back. You might even become infamous."

Luigi stood up and walked toward the window. Sam's arms hurt like hell, but it didn't stop him from grabbing the batteries with one hand and the bare end of the lamp cord with his other. When the wire was only inches from the battery, Sam yelled out, "Hey, wise guy!" When Luigi turned around, Sam peered into his eyes resolutely. "I'll see you in hell."

Luigi watched as Sam touched the lamp cord to the negative end of the C battery, knowing all too well what it meant. The positively charged blasting cap waited for its wake-up call deep inside one of the blocks of C4. Sam had calibrated the sequence to take several seconds, just enough time to enjoy the frantic look in Luigi's cantaloupe-sized eyes.

The four blocks of C4 exploded at 22,000 foot-pounds per second, causing a bright light, followed by a massive fireball that evaporated all the oxygen in the top two floors of the tower. The jolt knocked Misty off the rock wall, sending her crashing into the waiting arms of Miguel. The force knocked him to the ground. Miguel instinctively pushed Misty up against the side of the castle and lay on top of her. Massive chunks of stone crashed into the Caribbean, causing the seawater to shoot high into the air as if depth charges had just gone off beneath the water's surface. When the sky cleared, the water fell back to the sea, and the ringing in their ears subsided. Misty began screaming hysterically. Miguel covered her mouth with his hand and said in a consoling but firm voice, "Sam is gone, Misty. Nothing can bring him back."

The rest of the book deals with their escape from the Caribbean authorities and heading back to Argentina on a slow boat they leased. Misty is severely depressed, so Gabriella brings Rob and Amilla to see her with their new daughter. They ask Misty to be the little girl's godmother. Misty holds the baby tight to her chest, devouring her sweet innocence. Gary calls from Vegas with good news. The Captain and Mikey decide to go to Tahiti. Misty decided to retire from being the Black Widow Trainer, so Miguel and Monique decided to go to Tahiti with the Captain.

And Misty? The following is an excerpt from *Hanging by a Thread*:

The plane touched down at the airport at four in the afternoon. Misty was both anxious and excited, she wondered if she was doing the right thing. Misty looked the crowd over as she rode down the escalator to the luggage area, slightly disappointed when she didn't see the person she was looking for. Her anxiety overpowered her excitement, and her hands shook as she grabbed her luggage from the carousel.

You didn't think I was going to ruin the ending for you, did you?

After three books and a little less than three years, I knew the story was complete. Misty started as a flawed protagonist. Her character arc took 900 pages and three books to complete. There was nothing more to write, so I stopped writing. Until now, that is.

The Black Widow Trainer Screenplay

I hired a publisher, Victor Gulotta, to promote the upcoming release of *The Black Widow Trainer*. Victor hired a writer, Michael Borden, to write a synopsis of the script and my short bio. It required Michael to read the book. A week after the launch, Michael contacted me. He said that the entire time he read *The Black Widow Trainer*, he kept seeing a movie and approached me about writing a screenplay. After thinking it over, I thought it might be fun, and since I had more ideas for a sequel, I gave Michael the green light. Michael hired Francisca Matos, who had previously written a script that had been made into a movie.

Seeing my book turned into a professionally written screenplay was an exciting experience. Even better, the three of us worked and got along well. Everyone listened and respected the other persons' point of view. The challenge was to keep the storyline as close as possible to the book, while letting them have the freedom to do their craft. The book was my baby, and at first, I felt the pangs of a writer seeing the new content. I know how most authors might struggle, but fortunately, I quickly crossed from the creative side of my brain to the business side. Better to surround yourself with good people and give them leeway. All that matters is coming up with the best product in the end.

Michael has a brilliant mind for crisp, cutting dialogue full of sarcasm and wit. His writing style manifested itself in exchanges between Misty and her husband, Rob. Sharp-tongued but not brutal. A lover's spat that most people never let the outside world see. Francisca and Michael collaborated, and it was good having a woman's point of view. Francisca was great at giving the character more depth and creating backstories where needed.

The finished product was solid. I posted the screenplay on the Black List, a site where you can expose your script to the industry, and purchased three evaluations. They were favorable; two sevens and one six. At the time, I had no idea how good that was. All I kept thinking about was that if any script got an eight, everyone in the industry that used the Black List would be emailed the screenplay for review. It was that shiny nugget that had me reach for the brass ring. So, I paid for three more evaluations, awaiting my free pass. That turned out to be a big mistake. Now I was getting a six and several low scores. My average rating slipped, and I was heading in the wrong direction.

The basic critique was that Misty was unlikeable to many of the reviewers. The reviews that took place happened ten years ago. Flawed female protagonists were not in vogue, nor were leading female ladies. The bi-sexual relationship with Gabriella may have been too much at the time as well. And then there was Misty, who although never planning to, got swept off her feet by a handsome stranger in Hawaii. Misty had cheated on Rob, a nice guy but one that was in way over his head with such an attractive, free-spirited woman. I wondered how many of the paid reviews were done by women. Black List won't tell you anything about the reviewers, which is for their protection, and I understood.

The reviews gave us the feedback we needed to reinvent the script. Francisca developed a backstory of horrendous abuse by Misty's stepmother. We had no desire to change Misty's adventurous nature, hoping that maybe giving her an excuse would help. Michael and Francisca had a strong desire to develop the screenplay into one with more action. So, I turned them loose. Francisca and Michael went back and weaved the action into the early storyline, adding new characters and places along the way. Yet *The Black Widow Trainer* storyline remained the foundation. And the original characters remained the main characters, many making their way to the two sequel books and hopefully, screenplays. Yet we never had an agent, and I didn't realize at the time that without an agent on my Black List page to contact, the script was dead in the water.

By now, I had plowed ahead with *Captured Prey* and *Hanging by a Thread*. I lost interest and moved on. If it weren't for my good friend, David Solar, the script would still be a PDF collecting proverbial dust. David's agent, Elisa Celli, has made great strides with his screenplay, and at the time of writing, it looks like a movie is imminent. It would be wonderful if David hit such notoriety at a late stage in his life. But then it seems like just yesterday David and I practiced juggling three golf balls during slow days under the little red roof!

I'm happy to say Elisa is now my agent as well. We have strong interest from a producer in making *The Black Widow Trainer* into a movie. If/when a contract gets signed, I plan on moving forward with developing *Captured Prey* into a script and eventually *Hanging by a Thread*, should I be so lucky. The notoriety from a feature film would no doubt jumpstart book sales. If/when the first domino falls, I plan on going back and reworking the trilogy. My first goal would be to hire a female writer to tone down the sex scenes. I'm afraid my mind is just too imaginative and detailed.

I'm not interested in the fame and fortune aspect, should

it happen. But I have a strong desire to see the characters and storyline played out on the big screen. I've often said there is no way to describe the excitement and blessing of grandchildren. I imagine there is no way to explain to an author what it would feel like to see his imagination play out on the big screen. Those to events can only be experienced not explained.

The Credits

I've thought long and hard about this portion of the book. I realized that my entire book is a credit to everyone who shared my *long and winding journey*. I think there's a song in there, don't you? But a special shout-out goes to Roger Davidson and Wanda Polasek, who read every chapter as I laid it down. Their encouragement and interest in my project meant a lot. Roger was on many of my trips to do research. Wanda tirelessly edited my writing like a high school English teacher. Oh, the misspelled words. I've played around with the idea of misspelling Wanda's name in the book as a tease. Who knows, maybe I already have. And if the editors don't catch it, oh well, Wanda. Time will tell. Also, many thanks to Melissa Messer. Not sure my first book would have been accepted by a publisher without your help. And Richard Yount for selflessly researching the legal aspects in *Captured Prey*.

To my lovely and dear wife, Cathie. You have been by my side every step of the way. I wouldn't be surprised if some of those footsteps aren't you carrying me. Yet here we are! More in love with each other than ever. Life is a journey, honey, and we're still on the path. Can't wait to see what the future has in store for us.

To my children, Jack West Odanovich, Michelle Brooks Peterson, Amy Linnea Odanovich, and Stephen Harper Odanovich. It's been a long and winding road for us as well. I'm sorry I didn't give you the time you deserved while involved with all my business escapades. Yet, I came home every night and spent my time with the family. I wish I had spent more one-on-one time with you individually. I could have done more, but I still have plenty of time to make it up. I will leave you with this: *Happiness is when you realize your kids turned out to be genuinely good people.* Guess that makes me one happy guy.

My grandchildren, Sydney Brooks Peterson, Wynn Katherine Peterson, and my little buddy, Thayer James Peterson. You are too special to put into words. Listen to your father through your life, Stephen, as he is a good man and will guide you well. And your mom, of course.

To my sisters, Cheryl Robbins and Jan Charbeneau, I'm glad you will be able to read about my life while you were both out of state carving out your own lives. Jan, thank you for your loving support. And thank you, Denis, for catching my misspelled words. Cherry, you are steady as a rock. Be grateful Ray has been such a business success, and has provided you with the wherewithal to withstand the many challenges you have had to endure in your life. I'm sure God has a fast pass for your entry to heaven when the time comes.

And my dear departed parents, Stephen Michael Odanovich and Jacqueline (Jane) West Odanovich. You gave me my work ethic and taught me how to treat people. Your support and inspiration was immeasurable. Without my parents, I wouldn't have accomplished as much, I am sure. I owe you the sincerest gratitude and miss you dearly.

To Jeremy Gotwals, Grace Beck, Rebekah Spivey, and Victoria Stingo at Holon Publishing. Jeremy, your company reminds me of my early companies. Great team atmosphere, young, strong talent — and you are only in your thirties. I see great things for you and your company in the days ahead.

Wonderful life, wonderful wife, wonderful family, relatives, and friends! Who could ask for anything more?

God bless you all!

It's a wrap!

Craig's Record Factory Partners

Abraham, Nancy Norris
Aldridge, Danny
Bocanegra, Mary
Cadena, Dan
Carl, Sandi
Elliot, Jim
Emmord, Laura
Fandrich, Jeff
Gonzales, Yolanda
Gonzalez, Al
Hamilton, Bob
James, Liz
Janda, Nancy
Johnson, Ashley
Lakin, Mike (Frizby)
Martinez, Jaun
Martinez, Orlando
Mora, Denise
Mullinex, Rick

Najera, Robert
Najera, Tricia Norris
Norris, Bet
Norris, Jack (Cactus Jack)
Odanovich, Cathie Norris
Odanovich, Jane (Mrs O)
Odanovich, Steve (Mr O)
Roberson, Kooter (Talk Jock)
Salinas, Ernie
Seeds, Brenda
Simpson, Patti
Smith, Greg
Smith, Roy
Solar, David
Villarreal, Lilly
George
Pat
Susan

H-E-B Video Central Partners

Aaron, Claude
Almaguer, Jay
Alvarado, Lando
Anderson, Linda Gold
Appelt, Judy
Aschenbeck, Steve
Askew, Cecily
Babel, Tina
Baker, Brett
Barrera, Martin
Beitz, Barry
Benbele, C.K. Burleson
Black, Karen Mills
Blackwell Fuller, Theresa
Blackwell, Tracey
Blanco, Ben
Briones, Jerry
Briones, Tony
Brown , Kevin
Burkett, Shannon
Cadena, Andy
Camarillo, Paul
Cavazos, Peter
Ceppelin, Rub
Chapa, Lawrence
Collett, Ginger
Coonan, Debbie
Cortez, Irene
Cuevas, Raymond
Davidson, Roger
Davila, Lisias
Davila, Pat
Dean, Cathy
Delavergne, Denise
Delgado, Maryann Pinon

Diaz, Rosalie
Dolan, Guy
Escamilla, Leticia
Farias, Pat
Farias, Rosie
Feeny, Linda
Fick, Yolanda
Fierros, Philip
Frederick, Diana
Garcia, Patrice
Garner, Rob
Geoff Merritt
Glenn, Randy
Gonzales, Anthony
Gonzales, Antonio
Gonzales, Sabino
Griffin, Wayne
Hancock, Julie Morales
Hawk, Marcia
Hernandez, Debbie
Hernandez, Tina
Hill, Doug
Huron, Ruth
Jacko, Nanette
Jackson, Darren
Jaksha, Sandy
James, Liz
Jennings, Jon
Jiminez, Zorida
Klovstad, Diane
Klovstad, Kelly
Kuhn Cantu, Terri
Lawson, William
Legg, James
Lewis, Neal

Loera, Noel
Lopez, Juan
Luna, Connie
Maldonado, Yvonne
Markert, Alan
Martinez, Deeanna
Martinez, Jr., Cipiriano
Martinez, Juan
Martinez, Orlando
McChesney, Jennie
Mendez, James
Mitchell, Kenneth
Montalvo-Garza, Margaret
Mulinix, Rick
Najera, Robert
Navaira III, Louis
Neri, Armando
Ochoa, John
Ochoa, Melissa
Odanovich, Craig
Ojeda, Robert
Ortega, Oscar
Ortega, Robert
Patnoe, Clarence
Payne, Alan
Pelley, Jeremy
Pena, Terri
Perez, Luci
Perkins, Robert
Piner, Heather
Piner, Pete
Polasek, Wanda Knippa
Pope, Vera
Powers, Richard
Quintanilla, Gracie

Raef, Justin
Rankin, Shelly
Revett, Earl
Rodriguez, Eddie
Rodriguez, John
Rodriguez, Maria
Rodriguez, Ronald
Salter, Don
Sandoval, Pat
Schram, Rusty
Seago, Art
Seago, Doug
Seago, Ken
Seago, Rachelle
Sepulveda, Robert
Smarzek, Richard
Smith, Greg
Solar, Dave
Starnes Steve
Szymanski, Cathey
Tidwell, Lisa
Torres, Thomas
Trevino, Frances
Trevino, Leo
Turner, Pamela
Wagner, Tom
Ward, Beth
Wilson, Kimberly
Wood, Ava
Wright, Sarah Dee
Youngblood Smith, Karen
Zamora, Sheila

About the Author

Craig Odanovich grew up in Flour Bluff, Texas. In an era before Dairy Queen officially expanded their menu beyond dessert, Craig learned entrepreneurial principles working for the family-owned franchise. Later as a young music entrepreneur, Odanovich launched a successful record store: Craig's Record Factory. It was a time when neighborhood record stores were still a prime point of connection between popular music and the public. The experience augmented Criag's passion for music and prepared him for future business ventures.

Craig rose to the executive level in the early video rental industry. He competed neck-to-neck with Blockbuster and led growth for the regional grocery chain H-E-B. Craig continued to apply his skills towards building value in subsequent competitive business arenas until his retirement.

Not one to shy away from a new endeavor, Craig dove into writing. In two and a half years, he published the steamy adventure trilogy, the Black Widow Trainer. Throughout the many stages of his career, Odanovich maintained interest in popular music and film. Three decades of avidly collecting music and watching movies provided a wellspring of inspiration for the author.

Odanovich currently pursues his writing career in San Antonio, Texas. He and his wife, Cathie, have four children. Craig has many interests from family and grandkids, to sporting events and world affairs.

"After writing my trilogy I always said that if I wrote another book it would be more like The Old Man and the Sea. I didn't realize that old man would be me."

CPSIA information can be obtained
at www.ICGtesting.com
Printed in the USA
LVHW071925121121
703183LV00004BA/40